WWW.ZODIACSERVICES.NET

Presents

MBA BASICS IN 24 HOURS!

A SIMPLE HANDBOOK OF RETAIL MARKETING!

ADDITIONAL BOOK 5 – RETAIL MARKETING!

Life Grows With Us!

SIMPLE & EASY WAY TO UNDERSTAND THE BASICS OF BUSINESS ADMINISTRATION TOPICS EASILY IN SUMMARY AND KEYWORDS WITH 8 EFFECTIVE CHAPTERS & ADDITIONAL TOPICS!

By

G.R. Narasimhan

Welcome to Zodiac Services MBA chapters in brief with eight effective and additional special topics given as individual & additional books!

GOOD LUCK TO BE A BUSINESS ADMINISTRATOR!

Copyright © 2020 by **Narasimhan Ranganathan @ G. R. Narasimhan**

All rights reserved. No part of this book/e-book may be reproduced, distributed or transmitted in any form or by any means, including photocopying, recording or other electronic or mechanical methods, without the prior written permission of the author, except in the case of brief quotations embodied in critical reviews and certain other non-commercial uses permitted by copyright law. For permission requests, write to the author, addressed 'Attention: Author', at the address below.

Zodiac Services, Chennai, India

Get more contact details and numbers from:

www.zodiacservices.net [or] mail to info@zodiacservices.net

Ordering Information for hardcopies:

Quantity sales – Special discounts are available on quantity purchases by corporations, associations and others. For details, contact the author at the address above.

DEC 2020 – First Edition

Released and Published in India

****
Legal Disclaimer/ Notice

All the chapters, topics, discussions, statements, e-books/books and web contents including this MBA in 24 hours either online or offline are under business administration category. This guide is recommended to get simple understanding and guidance of bachelors or masters in business administration only. Readers are requested to apply their own knowledge or refer or consult their own tutors or masters before acting on any of the recommendations for examinations and related activities. Neither Zodiac services nor any of its promoters, members or author (if anyone) holds any responsibility of any losses/ liability incurred (if any/ if you end up in loss) by acting on the same as given to follow in presentations or examinations. We or Zodiac services, Chennai/head or branch offices anywhere in the world/global, are not responsible for, and will not compensate in any way for, any loss or damage related directly or indirectly from/to the information on this book/e-book. Thanks for your cooperation!

****

ABOUT THE AUTHOR

G.R. Narasimhan – Sr. Consultant for technology and business under **RNP - Zodiac Services Chennai** which serves the people in abroad study, alternative beliefs/therapies like astrological predictions, prayers, remedies, prasanam (divine words) and vedic guidance for short- or long-term problems, vaastu, numerology, gem stones, yantras, mantras or rituals (related areas), yoga, meditation, counselling and alternative therapies consulting. Business & education, soft skills/software/electronics & communication training & promotion, web designing, career counselling and Internet/online & social media marketing are additionally served. Assisting the entrepreneurship business for the above mentioned areas to serve better for the clients, **G.R. Narasimhan** also the author of few e-books called 'A Simple guide to Vedic Astrology', 'Inverted Universal Meditation & Engineering/production/production', 'Secrets of Equity Stocks to make Millions', 'Symbolic Meditation & Developing ESP' and many other (are already available in Amazon) having extended experience in IT + Management areas developed website and online marketing using different business strategies and continue the service very well to extend further including this 'MBA Basics in 24 Hours with Additional Topics – Retail Marketing and Questions & Answers' –specifically based on the business administration topics applied overall in the academic curriculum. With the continuous extraordinary ability and skills in research/study and experience, he is able to explain and train/assist others with extended support and guidance by counselling/consulting effectively.

Great thanks and good luck for everyone reading this book on 'MBA Basics in 24 Hours' with almost all the areas of basic business administration or career growth individually or as a group. For any queries and feedback, you can contact directly via email to info@zodiacservices.net, info@astroservices.in or astronara@gmail.com.

CONTENTS

Topics	Page Numbers
INTRODUCTION	5
CHAPTER -1 - AN OVER VIEW OF RETAIL	7
CHAPTER -2 - RETAIL FORMATS AND THEORIES OF RETAIL DEVELOPMENT	11
CHAPTER -3 - RETAIL IN INDIA [LIKE OTHERS]	18
CHAPTER -4 - RETAIL IN KEY REGIONS OF THE WORLD/GLOBAL	24
CHAPTER -5 - UNDERSTANDING THE RETAIL CONSUMER	28
CHAPTER- 6 - RETAIL STRATEGY	32
CHAPTER -7 - STORE SITE SELECTION	36
CHAPTER -8 - METHODS OF RETAIL EXPANSION	39
CHAPTER -9 - BASIS OF RETAIL MERCHANDISING	44
CHAPTER-10 - THE PROCESS OF MERCHANDISE PLANNING	48
CHAPTER-11 - METHODS OF MERCHANDISE PROCUREMENT	52
CHAPTER-12 - RETAIL PRICING AND EVALUATING MERCHANDISE PERFORMANCE	56
CHAPTER-13 THE DEVELOPMENT OF PRIVATE LABELS	59
CHAPTER-14 CATERGORY MANAGEMENT	62
CHAPTER-15 - HUMAN RESOURSE MANAGEMENT IN RETAIL- A STRATEGIC TOOL	68
CHAPTER-16 - RETAIL STORE OPERATIONS	72
CHAPTER-17 - THE LEGAL AND ETHICAL ASPECTS OF THE RETAIL BUSINESS	76
CHAPTER-18 - STORE DESIGN, LAYOUT AND VISUAL MERCHANDISING	81
CHAPTER-19 - MANAGING RETAIL INFRASTRUCTURE	85
CHAPTER-20 - SUPPLY CHAIN MANAGEMENT	90
CHAPTER-21 - UNDERSTANDING RETAIL VIABILITY	94
CHAPTER-22 – RETAIL MARKETING AND BRANDING	102
CHAPTER-23 - SERVICING THE RETAIL CUSTOMER	106
CHAPTER-24 - ROLE OF TECHNOLOGY IN RETAIL	110
CHAPTER-25 - THE CHANGING FACETS OF RETAIL	114
CONCLUSION	121

INTRODUCTION

Business Administration is the combination of different areas of skills in management. Managing and maintaining several departments or areas of activities described in a single umbrella or vertical called management of business administration. The following areas are the main topics or chapters for the discussion under business administration, mostly common for any bachelors or master's studies.

- Principles & Practices of Management
- Human Resource Management
- Financial Management
- Marketing Management
- Organisational Behaviour
- Managerial Economics
- Strategic Management
- Management Information Systems

Then there are several branches extended in business administration like foreign trade, global marketing, international business, social work, information technology, finance, human resources etc. These above eight topics considered to summarise and define important brief summary and keywords under which various chapters for each topic are given (published in Amazon).

This book covers the summaries and definitions of keywords for the topic 'Retail Marketing and Q & A discussions' with the following chapters.

AN OVER VIEW OF RETAIL, RETAIL FORMATS AND THEORIES OF RETAIL DEVELOPMENT, RETAIL IN INDIA [LIKE OTHERS], RETAIL IN KEY REGIONS OF THE WORLD/GLOBAL, UNDERSTANDING THE RETAIL CONSUMER, RETAIL STRATEGY, STORE SITE SELECTION, METHODS OF RETAIL EXPANSION, BASIS OF RETAIL MERCHANDISING, THE PROCESS OF MERCHANDISE PLANNING, METHODS OF MERCHANDISE PROCUREMENT, RETAIL PRICING AND EVALUATING MERCHANDISE PERFORMANCE, THE DEVELOPMENT OF PRIVATE LABELS, CATERGORY MANAGEMENT, HUMAN RESOURCE MANAGEMENT IN RETAIL- A STRATEGIC TOOL, RETAIL STORE OPERATIONS, THE LEGAL AND ETHICAL ASPECTS OF THE RETAIL BUSINESS, STORE DESIGN, LAYOUT AND VISUAL MERCHANDISING, MANAGING RETAIL INFRASTRUCTURE, SUPPLY CHAIN MANAGEMENT, UNDERSTANDING RETAIL VIABILITY, RETAIL MARKETING AND BRANDING, SERVICING THE RETAIL CUSTOMER, ROLE OF TECHNOLOGY IN RETAIL, THE CHANGING FACETS OF RETAIL.

Some of the chapters given with examples of Indian economy/trading/retail/service-related terms. But readers must understand the concepts of their own country/nation's business & economy and other areas. Most of the answers are gathered from varies online/ offline resources and in turn makes life easier for the people to prepare for any exams or case studies.

As it has high level of contents in brief which can be covered in three hours maximum, readers can read other books from different authors to gain in-depth knowledge of the given business management and administration. This book gives quick glance & easy go chapters for any situation like interview, short answering and overall explanation to present others. Good Luck!

CHAPTER -1 - AN OVER VIEW OF RETAIL

SUMMARY

LO 1 Retail is the final stage of any economic activity. By virtue of this fact, retail occupies an important place in the world/global economy. While various definitions of the word 'retail' exist, retailing may be understood as the final step in the distribution of merchandise for consumption by the end consumers. Put simply, any firm that sells products to the final consumer is performing the function of retailing. It is necessary to understand that in the complex world/global of trade today, retail would include not only goods, but also services which may be provided to the end consumer.

LO 2 The retailer is a link between the producer and the consumer and also a channel member. Today, retail has emerged as a separate function by itself. Several reasons for the same exist, the primary ones being the retailer's proximity to the consumer and the rise of consumerism. Growth of technology and the arrival of the internet have made it possible for business to develop across geographies at either business-to-business or B2B and business-to-consumer or B2C levels. This has not only enhanced the economics of scale available, but also made it easier to enter the retail market.

LO 3 The need to grow not only nationally, but also internationally has led to the field of retail witnessing many a merger. The significance of retail is apparent, not only from its contribution to various economies, but also by the level of employment generated by the industry/sector. In India, where organized retail is just, beginning to make its presence felt, it already contributes close to 6-7% of the employment. In the developed markets, organized retail controls a significantly higher portion of trade as compared to that of in a country/nation like India.

LO 4 The emergence of new markets and the empowered consumer is a key challenge faced by the retailers. Global competition, global and educated customers demanding more product information, limited brand loyalty are the realities of retail in the world/global today. The term, the customer is the king, is more relevant today than ever before as it is the customer who drives the sale, and in effect the retail operation. As consumer lifestyles change and an increasing section of the population works from home, the method of shopping will also change. Channels of distribution will blur, and the internet/online will emerge as a powerful channel of distribution, and mobile commerce may soon become a reality. Retailers will have to think of being present across channels of distribution and across geographies to ensure growth.

LO 5 Retail is a people-centric industry/sector, and 1s one industry/sector which simultaneously can expose you to many skills and disciplines. It offers many choices in terms of a career, chief among them are, Buying and Merchandising, Marketing, Store Operations, Sales, Finance, Human Resources, Technology and e-commerce, Visual Merchandising and Supply Chain Management and Logistics.

KEY TERMS

1. Retail
2. Marketing
3. Consumerism
4. Private labels
5. Global retail
6. Empowered consumer
7. Buying and merchandising
8. Store operations
9. Visual merchandising
10. Supply chain management
11. Logistics management

Review Questions

1. What is 'retail and what is the significance of retail as an industry/sector?

Ans- Retail is the final stage of any economic activity. By virtue of this fact, retail occupies an important place in the world/global economy. While various definitions of the word 'retail' exist, retailing may be understood as the final step in the distribution of merchandise for consumption by the end consumers. Put simply, any firm that sells products to the final consumer is performing the function of retailing. It is necessary to understand that in the complex world/global of trade today, retail would include not only goods, but also services which may be provided to the end consumer.

2. What are the functions performed by a retailer?

Ans- The retailer is a link between the producer and the consumer and also a channel member. Today, retail has emerged as a separate function by itself. Several reasons for the same exist, the primary ones being the retailer's proximity to the consumer and the rise of consumerism. Growth of technology and the arrival of the internet/online have made it possible for business to develop across geographies at either business-to-business or B2B and business-to-consumer or B2C levels. This has not only enhanced the economies of scale available, but also made it easier to enter the retail market.

3. Why has the retailer emerged as a leader in the marketing channel?

Ans- The need to grow not only nationally, but also internationally has led to the field of retail witnessing many a merger. The significance of retail is apparent, not only from its contribution to various economies, but also by the level of employment generated by the industry/sector. In India, where organized retail is just, beginning to make its presence felt, it already contributes close to 6-7% of the employment. In the developed markets, organized retail controls a significantly higher portion of trade as compared to that of in a country/nation like India.

4. What are the issues facing global retailers and how can they overcome the same?

Ans- The emergence of new markets and the empowered consumer is a key challenge faced by the retailers. Global competition, global and educated customers demanding more product information, limited brand loyalty are the realities of retail in the world/global today. The term, the customer is the king, is more relevant today than ever before as it is the customer who drives the sale, and in effect the retail operation. As consumer lifestyles change and an increasing section of the population works from home, the method of shopping will also change. Channels of distribution will blur, and the internet will emerge as a powerful channel of distribution, and mobile commerce may soon become a reality. Retailers will have to think of being present across channels of distribution and across geographies to ensure growth.

5. What are the different functions in which a career in the retail sector is possible?

Ans- Retail is a people-centric industry, and 1s one industry which simultaneously can expose you to many skills and disciplines. It offers many choices in terms of a career, chief among them are, Buying and Merchandising, Marketing, Store Operations, Sales, Finance, Human Resources, Technology and e-commerce, Visual Merchandising and Supply Chain Management and Logistics.

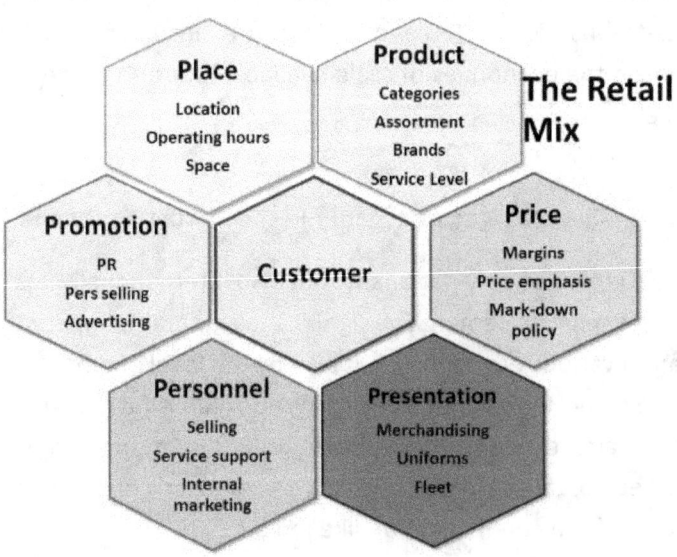

CHAPTER -2 - RETAIL FORMATS AND THEORIES OF RETAIL DEVELOPMENT

SUMMARY

LO1 The origins of retail are as old as trade itself. Barter was the oldest form of trade. The development of trading is intimately associated with social developments over the ages. Two important developments of the eighteenth century the development of railroads and telegraphs largely affected the growth of the retail trade.

LO 2 The theories developed to explain the process of retail development revolve around the importance of competitive pressures, the investments m organizational capabilities and the creation of a sustainable competitive advantage. This requires the implementation of strategic planning by retail organizations.
Retail development can also be looked at from the theoretical perspective. No single theory can be universally applicable or acceptable, the application of each theory varies from market to market depending on the level of maturity and the socio-economic conditions in that market

LO 3 The theories of retail development revolve around importance of competitive pressures, investment in organizational capabilities and developing sustainable advantage. They are broadly classified ratio: Environment theory, Cyclical theory and Conflictual theory.

LO 4 The industrial revolution necessitated dramatic changes on the retail front. The increase in urbanization meant that consumers were now clustered m smaller geographic areas. This led to the emergence of shops, to serve the needs of the locals. The industrial revolution saw the retailers evolving in new methods of operation. Retail evolved in many ways over the twentieth century with the emergence of self service, super markets, discount stores and convenience stores. As the needs of the consumers grew and changed, one saw the emergence of commodity specialized mass merchandisers in the 1970s. The seventies also were witness to the use of technology entering retail sector with the introduction of the barcode.

Specialty chains developed in the 1980s as did the large shopping malls. A business model is the manner in which a business chooses to serve its customers and stakeholders. In retail a business model would dictate the product and/or services offered by the retailer, the pricing policy that he adopts the communication that he follows to reach out to his customers and the size, look and the location of his retail store. This is termed in retail as a format in which the retailer operates.

KEY TERMS

1. Department stores
2. Supermarkets
3. Self service
4. Specialty stores
5. Cyclical theory
6. Retail life cycle
7. Shopping malls
8. Conflictual theory
9. Category killer
10. Hypermarkets
11. Environmental theory
12. Scrambled merchandising
13. Non-store retail
14. Service retail

REVIEW QUESTIONS

1. Discuss the impact of economic and sociological changes on the evolution of retail formats.

Ans- The origins of retail are as old as trade/exchange itself. Barter was the oldest form of trade/exchange. The development of trading is intimately associated with social developments over the ages. Two important developments of the eighteenth century the development of railroads and telegraphs largely affected the growth of the retail trade/exchange.

2. What is the 'retail life cycle? Explain with an example.

Ans- The theories developed to explain the process of retail development revolve around the importance of competitive pressures, the investments m organization/companyal capabilities and the creation of a sustainable competitive advantage. This requires the implementation of strategic planning by retail organization/companys.

3. Discuss the applicability of the retail life cycle in the Indian context.

Ans- Retail development can also be looked at from the theoretical perspective. No single theory can be universally applicable or acceptable, the application of each theory varies from market to market depending on the level of maturity and the socio-economic conditions in that market.

4. What are the reasons that have caused an increase in the popularity of the non-store retail formats to develop?

Ans- The industrial revolution necessitated dramatic changes on the retail front. The increase in urbanization meant that consumers were now clustered m smaller geographic areas. This led to the emergence of shops, to serve the needs of the locals. The industrial revolution saw the retailers evolving in new methods of operation. Retail evolved in many ways over the twentieth century with the emergence of self service, super markets, discount stores and convenience stores. As the needs of the consumers grew and changed, one saw the emergence of commodity specialized mass merchandisers in the 1970s. The seventies also were witness to the use of technology entering retail sector with the introduction of the barcode. Specialty chains developed in the 1980s as did the large shopping malls. A business model is the manner in which a business chooses to serve its customers and stakeholders.

In retail a business model would dictate the product and/or services offered by the retailer, the pricing policy that he adopts the communication that he follows to reach out to his customers and the size, look and the location of his retail store. This is termed in retail as a format in which the retailer operates.

5. What are the challenges that will be faced by a concept like airport retailing in India?

Ans- A number of factors have been responsible for the development of airport retailing in India. In recent years, passenger traffic has gone up exponentially with a number of low-cost airlines emerging on the scene, thereby giving way to a large captive consumer base right at the airport itself, seven days a week. Besides, the time spent by passengers at airports has increased due to early check-in times set by airlines owing to security and operational concerns, providing them with the opportunity to visit retail stores. Maximum shopping is done by people in the window between clearing the security-immigration desks and boarding the aircraft.

Thus, it made sense for the retailers to be present in an airport, more so since there is a shortage of quality retail space with high visibility in India. Further, factors such as evolving consumer attitudes, attractive real estate, conducive regulatory environment, economic environment and the overall ecosystem have fueled its growth. This has increased retail opportunities; thereby leading airports to develop retail as an integral part of operations rather than pushing the segment away in low-visibility corners.

6. Explain the following terms with Indian examples.

a. Hypermarket
b. Supermarket
c. Discount stores
d. Dollar stores
e. Airport retailing
f. Leased departments
g. Off price retailers

Answers:

a. Hypermarket
The word hypermarket is derived from the hypermarche which is a combination of a supermarket and a department store, this retail business format has evolved since its invention by retailer Carrefour in Sainte-Geneviève-des-Bois near Paris in the year 1963.

A retail store with a sales area of over 2,500 sqm, with at least 35o of selling space devoted to non-grocery products is termed as a hypermarket. I he stores Occupy an area which ranges anywhere between 80.000 and 2,20,000 sq ft and offer a variety of food and non-food products clothes, jewellery, hardware, sports equipment, cycles, motor accessories, books, CDs. DVDs Videos, TVs, electrical equipment, computers and com supermarket, discount &warehouse
retailing principles.

b. Supermarket
Supermarkets: Morrisons (1899) and Sainsbury's (1869) in the UK and Groupe Casino (1898) in Europe all started as stores selling fresh foods grocery products and could be termed as the earliest supermarkets. Tesco was founded in 1919 by Jack Cohen as a group of market stalls, The Tesco name first appeared in 1924, after Cohen purchased a shipment of tea from T. E Stockwell and combined those initials with the first two letters of his surname, and the first Tesco store opened in 1929 in Burnt Oak, Barnet. His business expanded rapidly, and by 1939 he had over 100 Tesco stores across the country/nation.

In 1930, Michael Cullen, opened the first King Kullen store, widely cited as America's first supermarket. King Kullen was located in a warehouse on the fringe of New York City, and offered ample free parking and additional concessions in a bazaar-like atmosphere. Merchandise was sold out of packing cartons and little attention was paid to décor. The emphasis was on volume, with this one store projected to do the volume of up to 100 conventional chain stores. The volume and the no frills approach resulted in considerably lower prices. The supermarket, as it came to be known, was initially a phenomenon of independents and small, regional chains.

Supermarkets are large, low cost, low margin, high volume self-service operations designed to meet the needs for food, groceries and other non-food items. This format was at the forefront of the grocery revolution, and today controls more than 30% of the grocery market in many Countries.

c. Discount stores
Discount department stores, ranging from 80,000 sqft to 130,000 sqft, offer a wide variety of merchandise including automotive parts and services, house wares, home furnishings, apparel and beauty aids.

d. Dollar stores
A traditional format that not sells 20-80 per cent of groceries and other consumables products at discounted prices.

e. Airport retailing
Gone is the age where airports were passenger processors, the time when travelling was just a hassle with passengers moaning and complaining about long waits, dull surroundings. We are now in the era where airports are focusing on retail to convert airports into exciting, energized business and retail/entertainment centers-as well as transportation hubs.
Airports in many cities of the world/global, serve as mini shopping plazas for the traveler, while the trend is yet to catch on in India. Dramatic changes swept airport retailing when long-term, 20-to-30-year concession contracts began expiring. It made airports realize more and more that with capital investment, good customer service

and good pricing, plus a little imagination, they could generate some attractive revenue.

f. Leased departments

Leased departments are also termed as shop-in-shops. When a section of a department in a retail store is leased/rented to an outside party it is termed as a leased department. A leased department within the stores is a good method available to the retailer for expanding his product offering to the customers. In India, many large department stores operate their perfumes and cosmetics counters in this manner. Anew trend emerging in Indian retail is that of larger retail chains setting up smaller retail outlets or counters in high traffic areas like malls, department stores multiplexes and public places like airports and railway
stations, these stores display only a fraction of the merchandise/products sold in the anchor stores. Their main aim is being available to the consumer near his place of work or home.

g. Off price retailers

Off price retailers sell the merchandise at less than retail prices. Off-price retailers buy manufacturers seconds, Overruns, oft seasons at a deep discount. The merchandise may be in odd sizes, unpopular colors or with minor detects. Of price retail stores may be to manufacturer owned or may be owned by a specialty or departmental store. These outlets are usually seen by the parent company as a means of increasing the business. The factory outlets in case the manufacturer owns them may stock only company merchandise. Examples of these include Pantaloon Factory Outlets, Levi s Factory Outlets, etc. On the other hand, off price retailers owned by the specialty or departmental store may sell merchandise from the parent company as well as merchandise acquired from other retailers. This format largely depends on volume sales to make money.

CHAPTER-3 - RETAIL IN INDIA [LIKE OTHERS]

SUMMARY

LO1 A look at the landscape of most of the cities in India shows the rapid pace of change. This change is a reflection of the changes in the Indian consumer, his lifestyle and his habits. Formats new to the Indian marketplace have emerged rapidly over the past five years. There is little doubt that retail in India is reviving up for an existing phase ahead.

LO 2,3 The origins of retail can be traced back to barter trade/exchange. Various formats have evolved over the past thousand years and have been influenced by social and economic developments of the era. Retailers today are no longer dependent on manufacturers to sell what is available but have emerged as the new leaders in the marketing channel. Since Independence retail in India has evolved to support the unique needs of our country/nation given its size and complexity. In India, Retail is the new buzzword. While it has not as yet been accorded the status of an industry/sector, it is witness to a large number of formats emerging in the market at a very fast pace. Changes in lifestyles, family structures, living spaces, aspirations and a corresponding rise in income levels have changed the consumer dynamics of the country/nation in ways unimaginable even 10 years ago.

The booming Indian economy led India's large conglomerates to venture into retail. While many brands have been drawn to the Indian market it is also true that a few brands exited the market. The growth of malls and the advent of specialized malls like DLF Emporio saw the advent of global luxury brands like Louis Vuitton, Cartier, Gucci, Jimmy Choo, Dior, Hugo Boss Burberry, Tumi and Hackett to name a few entered the country/nation.

The rising internet/online penetration has resulted in an increase in the number of people going online in the past few years. The introduction of modern communication technologies including mobile and broadband connections, 3G and 4G connections are making it easier for Indians to transact online. Several global and local brands such as Puma, GKB Opticals, Reebok, Shopper stop, and Fast Track are increasingly adopting e-tailing to expand their customer base, particularly in small Indian cites, without opening many brick and mortar stores.

LO 4 Retail transformation in India is not restricted to the metro cities but has rapidly spread to smaller cities and towns. The key drivers of change in India are the economic growth, the booming Indian middle class, favorable demographics, the changing family structure, changing consumption habits and rapid urbanization.

LO 5 The retail trade/exchange in India is highly fragmented in nature and it is often remarked that retail in India is nascent and mostly unorganized. What one sees of the retail sector in India is just the tip of the iceberg. As retail is not regarded as an industry/sector in India it is difficult to get a correct picture of the size of this sector. The local bania or kirana store, the paanwala, and the vegetable vendor who are very much a part of the Indian retail landscape is termed by many as the unorganized sector. Many of the business models have been in existence since time immemorial, and at the same time have a presence across the country/nation. At the top of the market hierarchy are mandis, which owe their development partly to government policies on agricultural marketing. Unlike the regulated markets, there are also unregulated markets known as haats, peta, angadi, hatwart, shandies, chindwes or painths. A haat is a periodic market which exists typically at a village level. Another prominent feature of the Indian rural life is a mela.

LO 6 Some of the challenges faced by retailers in India include the lack of recognition as an industry/sector hampers the availability of finance to the existing and new players. Real estate prices in some cities in India are among the highest in the world/global. In addition to the high cost of real estate, the sector also faces very high stamp duties on transfer of property- varies from state to state. Poor roads, the lack of a cold chain infrastructure hampers the development of food and fresh grocery retail in India and multiple and complex taxation system.

KEY TERMS

1. Unorganised sector
2. Organised retail
3. Modern trade/exchange
4. Public distribution system
5. Mandi
6. Canteen stores department
7. Melas
8. Haat
9. Economic growth
10. Agricultural produce marketing committee
11. Demographics
12. Urbanilsation

Review Questions

1. What are the reasons for the growth of organized retail in India?

Ans- A look at the landscape of most of the cities in India shows the rapid pace of change. This change is a reflection of the changes in the Indian consumer, his lifestyle and his habits. Formats new to the Indian marketplace have emerged rapidly over the past five years. There is little doubt that retail in India is reviving up for an existing phase ahead.

2 What is the socio-economic impact of retail development in India?

Ans- The origins of retail can be traced back to barter trade. Various formats have evolved over the past thousand years and have been influenced by social and economic developments of the era. Retailers today are no longer dependent on manufacturers to sell what is available but have emerged as the new leaders in the marketing channel. Since Independence retail in India has evolved to support the unique needs of our country/nation given its size and complexity. In India, Retail is the new buzzword. While it has not as yet been accorded the status of an industry, it is witness to a large number of formats emerging in the market at a very fast pace.

Changes in lifestyles, family structures, living spaces, aspirations and a corresponding rise in income levels have changed the consumer dynamics of the country/nation in ways unimaginable even 10 years ago.

The booming Indian economy led India's large conglomerates to venture into retail. While many brands have been drawn to the Indian market it is also true that a few brands exited the market. The growth of malls and the advent of specialized malls like DLF Emporio saw the advent of global luxury brands like Louis Vuitton, Cartier, Gucci, Jimmy Choo, Dior, Hugo Boss Burberry, Tumi and Hackett to name a few entered the country/nation.

The rising internet/online penetration has resulted in an increase in the number of people going online in the past few years. The introduction of modern communication technologies including mobile and broadband connections, 3G and 4G connections are making it easier for Indians to transact online. Several global and local brands such as Puma, GKB Opticals, Reebok, Shopper stop, and Fast Track are increasingly adopting e-tailing to expand their customer base, particularly in small Indian cites, without opening many brick and mortar stores.

3. The supply chain in food distribution in India is inefficient. Can organized retail help in removing these inefficiencies? Explain how this can take place.

Ans- Some of the challenges faced by retailers in India include the lack of recognition as an industry/sector hampers the availability of finance to the existing and new players. Real estate prices in some cities in India are among the highest in the world/global. In addition to the high cost of real estate, the sector also faces very high stamp duties on transfer of property- varies from state to state. Poor roads, the lack of a cold chain infrastructure hampers the development of food and fresh grocery retail in India and multiple and complex taxation system.

4. Keeping in mind the developments happening on the Indian retail scene, what is the need of the hour for Indian retailers?

Ans- Retail transformation in India is not restricted to the metro cities but has rapidly spread to smaller cities and towns. The key drivers of change in India are the economic growth, the booming Indian middle class, favorable demographics, the changing family structure, changing consumption habits and rapid urbanization.

The retail trade/exchange in India is highly fragmented in nature and it is often remarked that retail in India is nascent and mostly unorganized. What one sees of the retail sector in India is just the tip of the iceberg. As retail is not regarded as an industry/sector in India it is difficult to get a correct picture of the size of this sector. The local bania or kirana store, the paanwala, and the vegetable vendor who are very much a part of the Indian retail landscape is termed by many as the unorganized sector. Many of the business models have been in existence since time immemorial, and at the same time have a presence across the country/nation. At the top of the market hierarchy are mandis, which owe their development partly to government policies on agricultural marketing. Unlike the regulated markets, there are also unregulated markets known as haats, peta, angadi, hatwart, shandies, chindwes or painths. A haat is a periodic market which exists typically at a village level. Another prominent feature of the Indian rural life is a mela.

Some of the challenges faced by retailers in India include the lack of recognition as an industry/sector hampers the availability of finance to the existing and new players. Real estate prices in some cities in India are among the highest in the world/global. In addition to the high cost of real estate, the sector also faces very high stamp duties on transfer of property- varies from state to state. Poor roads, the lack of a cold chain infrastructure hampers the development of food and fresh grocery retail in India and multiple and complex taxation system.

5. Given the growth of various sectors in Indian retail, which sector is likely to grow faster than the other sectors till 2020? Why?

Ans- The retail trade/exchange in India is highly fragmented in nature and it is often remarked that retail in India is nascent and mostly unorganized. What one sees of the retail sector in India is just the tip of the iceberg. As retail is not regarded as an industry/sector in India it is difficult to get a correct picture of the size of this sector. The local bania or kirana store, the paanwala, and the vegetable vendor who are very much a part of the Indian retail landscape is termed by many as the unorganized sector. Many of the business models have been in existence since time immemorial, and at the same time have a presence across the country/nation. At the top of the market hierarchy are mandis, which owe their development partly to government policies on agricultural marketing. Unlike the regulated markets, there are also unregulated markets known as haats, peta, angadi, hatwart, shandies, chindwes or painths. A haat is a periodic market which exists typically at a village level. Another prominent feature of the Indian rural life is a mela.

Some of the challenges faced by retailers in India include the lack of recognition as an industry/sector hampers the availability of finance to the existing and new players. Real estate prices in some cities in India are among the highest in the world/global. In addition to the high cost of real estate, the sector also faces very high stamp duties on transfer of property- varies from state to state. Poor roads, the lack of a cold chain infrastructure hampers the development of food and fresh grocery retail in India and multiple and complex taxation system.

CHAPTER-4 - RETAIL IN KEY REGIONS OF THE WORLD/GLOBAL

SUMMARY

LO 1 World/global over, the retail industry/sector is increasingly becoming more complex and is changing at a rapid pace. In this consumer-driven industry/sector, retailers are increasingly constrained in their ability to grow and maintain profit margins as a result of high operating expenses, market saturation, the rise of multi-channel buying, an ageing population, less affluent buyers, diminished consumer loyal and the rise of digital media which influences influence purchase decisions. The dominance in trade/exchange is largely based on the purchasing power m the economy However, the change in the demographic break up in the home countries and the changing economic power of the new and emerging markets is now leading many {international retailers to consider expansion into new markets.

LO 2 The United States of America is a dominant force in the world/global of retail. Geographically located between Canada in the north and Mexico in the south, the USA is the largest importer in the world/global and the third largest exporter. Retailing is the second largest sector in the US, both in terms of the number of establishments and number of employees. The country/nation is, however, now faced with an ageing population and the shrinking of the typical American family.

LO 3 'Europe' aka the European Union, is made up of a diverse range of individual markets of very different size and market potential. A dominant feature of European retailing is the level of internationalization. The European retail landscape has a wide spectrum of brands like Zara, Mango, H & M and it is also home to no frills discounters like Aldi and Lidl.

LO 4 The Asia-Pacific as a region is significantly different from the rest of the world/global in terms of culture, food habits and lifestyles. Geographic proximity goes hand-in-hand with great diversity in language, tradition, culture, preferences and behaviours. Modern retail is playing an increasingly prominent role in shaping the retail landscape across this region. From being typified by small, independent retail outlets (i.e., traditional retailing), Asia Pacific economies are being rapidly transformed by a large number of modern trade/exchange formats which now dot these economies.

LO 5 The traditional retail landscape in the UAE has evolved from the souk (traditional bazaar) culture to a more organized retail. Shopping events in Dubai, such as DSS, the DSF and Dubai Duty-Free (DDF), are major contributors to the UAE's retail industry/sector. The successful marketing of Dubai in particular as a global leisure and shopping destination has had a major impact on the Emirate's retail scene

LO 6 As in the majority of other Latin American countries, Chile is also becoming increasingly urban, not only in the country/nation's major metropolis but also wm other provincial and second-tier cities.

KEY TERMS
1. **Purchasing power**
2. **Ageing population**
3. **Economic trends**
4. **Consumer driven**
5. **Geographic proximity**
6. **Souk**
7. **Multichannel retail**
8. **Internationalization**
9. **Fragmented**

Review questions

1. What are the factors that have led to retailers expanding beyond their home countries?

Ans- World/global over, the retail industry/sector is increasingly becoming more complex and is changing at a rapid pace. In this consumer-driven industry/sector, retailers are increasingly constrained in their ability to grow and maintain profit margins as a result of high operating expenses, market saturation, the rise of multi-channel buying, an ageing population, less affluent buyers, diminished consumer loyal and the rise of digital media which influences influence purchase decisions. The dominance in trade/exchange is largely based on the purchasing power m the economy However, the change in the demographic break up in the home countries and the changing economic power of the new and emerging markets is now leading many {international retailers to consider expansion into new markets.

2. How has retail development differed in parts of Asia as compared to the United States of America?

Ans- The United States of America is a dominant force in the world/global of retail. Geographically located between Canada in the north and Mexico in the south, the USA is the largest importer in the world/global and the third largest exporter. Retailing is the second largest sector in the US, both in terms of the number of establishments and number of employees. The country/nation is, however, now faced with an ageing population and the shrinking of the typical American family.

3. Write a short note on a few important European retailers.

Ans-3 'Europe' aka the European Union, is made up of a diverse range of individual markets of very different size and market potential. A dominant feature of European retailing is the level of internationalization. The European retail landscape has a wide spectrum of brands like Zara, Mango, H & M and it is also home to no frills discounters like Aldi and Lidl.

4 Give a detailed account on the retailing business in Asia-Pacific, Australia and UAE.

Ans- The Asia-Pacific as a region is significantly different from the rest of the world/global in terms of culture, food habits and lifestyles. Geographic proximity goes hand-in-hand with great diversity in language, tradition, culture, preferences and behaviors. Modern retail is playing an increasingly prominent role in shaping the retail landscape across this region. From being typified by small, independent retail outlets (i.e., traditional retailing), Asia Pacific economies are being rapidly transformed by a large number of modern trade/exchange formats which now dot these economies.

The traditional retail landscape in the UAE has evolved from the souk (traditional bazaar) culture to a more organized retail. Shopping events in Dubai, such as DSS, the DSF and Dubai Duty-Free (DDF), are major contributors to the UAE's retail industry/sector. The successful marketing of Dubai in particular as a global leisure and shopping destination has had a major impact on the Emirate's retail scene.

5 What kind of retail development has taken place in Latin America?

Ans- As in the majority of other Latin American countries, Chile is also becoming increasingly urban, not only in the country/nation's major metropolis but also in other provincial and second-tier cities.

CHAPTER -5 - UNDERSTANDING THE RETAIL CONSUMER

SUMMARY

LO 1 Consumer Behavior is a process of understanding why a consumer makes a purchase, when he buys if, where does he buy the products and the frequency of the purchase. It helps one understand the why when, where and how often of a purchase decision.

LO 2 As the behavior of retail shoppers varies across markets, it becomes necessary to understand what drives consumers in order to be able to provide the right range of merchandise to the consumers. The existence of the customer is integral to the existence of the retailer. The ability to understand consumers is the key to developing a successful retail strategy. A key factor in understanding customers is identifying the customers for the product or service i.e., the target segment and the demographics of this segment, their needs and buying behavior.

LO3 Understanding the reasons for consumers choosing of patronizing a store is important for the retailer. Typically, a consumer goes through various stages before making a buying decision which include identification of the need for the product or service, the search for information and evaluating the alternatives and finally making the purchase decision. The key factors influencing consumer behavior are the personality of the consumer, his lifestyle and the social class that he is a part of and the cultural, family and household influences. The experience gained during and after the purchase leads to satisfaction or dissatisfaction with that particular store. The customer assimilates the experience that the customer has had while shopping, post purchase satisfaction or dissatisfaction.

LO 4 Recognition of the need for a product or a service is the first stage that may lead to a consumer buying. The need may be psychological or functional in the next stage, the consumer seeks information about the product and the place where he can make the purchase. Depending on the criteria important to him, the consumer evaluates the various options available and narrows down the choice to a few stores where he may make the purchase. A buying decision is then made. The experience during and after

the purchase leads to satisfaction or dissatisfaction with that particular store.
In a short span of a little over 10 years, the change that has occurred in the Indian consumer is phenomenal. Liberalization and steady economic growth have been the main factors, which have driven this change.

LO 5 Retail strategy is largely information based. The gathering and analysis of data relevant to the retailer Is done by market research. From the retailers perspective, market research needs to be done prior to as well as after setting up of a retail store. The information needed at both stages varies significantly. In a world/global of increasing competition, research can aid the retailer in satisfying the customer and thereby build loyalty.

KEY TERMS

1. Family life cycle
2. Demographics
3. Consumer decision-making process
4. Lifestyle
5. Culture
6. Social class
7. Secondary data
8. Primary data
9. Family and household influences
10. Focus group discussion
11. Accompanied observation

Review Questions

1. Who is a 'consumer? Why is a consumer important to a retailer?

Ans- Consumer Behavior is a process of understanding why a consumer makes a purchase, when he buys if, where does he buy the products and the frequency of the purchase. It helps one understand the why when, where and how often of a purchase decision.

As the behavior of retail shoppers varies across markets, it becomes necessary to understand what drives consumers in order to be able to provide the right range of merchandise to the consumers.

The existence of the customer is integral to the existence of the retailer. The ability to understand consumers is the key to developing a successful retail strategy. A key factor in understanding customers is identifying the customers for the product or service i.e., the target segment and the demographics of this segment, their needs and buying behavior.

2. What are the factors that affect the buying behavior of a retail shopper?

Ans- The key factors influencing consumer behavior are the personality of the consumer, his lifestyle and the social class that he is a part of and the cultural, family and household influences. The experience gained during and after the purchase leads to satisfaction or dissatisfaction with that particular store. The customer assimilates the experience that the customer has had while shopping, post purchase satisfaction or dissatisfaction.

3. What is the consumer buying process'? Does this process vary for convenience products and for high priced, high involvement products?

Ans- Recognition of the need for a product or a service is the first stage that may lead to a consumer buying. The need may be psychological or functional in the next stage, the consumer seeks information about the product and the place where he can make the purchase. Depending on the criteria important to him, the consumer evaluates the various options available and narrows down the choice to a few stores where he may make the purchase. A buying decision is then made. The experience during and after the purchase leads to satisfaction or dissatisfaction with that particular store.

In a short span of a little over 10 years, the change that has occurred in the Indian consumer is phenomenal. Liberalization and steady economic growth have been the main factors, which have driven this change.

4. How has the Indian consumer changed in the past decade? What are the challenges that the new consumer poses for the retailer?

Ans- Understanding the reasons for consumers choosing of patronizing a store is important for the retailer. Typically a consumer goes through various stages before making a buying decision which include identification of the need for the product or service, the search for information and evaluating the alternatives and finally making the purchase decision.

5. What are the developments in retail that have come about as a consequence of the changed Indian consumer?

Ans As the behavior of retail shoppers varies across markets, it becomes necessary to understand what drives consumers in order to be able to provide the right range of merchandise to the consumers.

The existence of the customer is integral to the existence of the retailer. The ability to understand consumers is the key to developing a successful retail strategy. A key factor in understanding customers is identifying the customers for the product or service i.e., the target segment and the demographics of this segment, their needs and buying behavior.

6. Why is research essential to a retailer?

Ans- Retail strategy is largely information based. The gathering and analysis of data relevant to the retailer Is done by market research. From the retailers perspective, market research needs to be done prior to as well as after setting up of a retail store. The information needed at both stages varies significantly. In a world/global of increasing competition, research can aid the retailer in satisfying the customer and thereby build loyalty.

CHAPTER-6 - RETAIL STRATEGY

SUMMARY

LO 1 Increased competition and the expansion of retail markets have forced many retailers to rethink their strategies. Various definitions of strategy prevail and according to Henry Mintzberg people use "strategy" in several different ways, the most common being the one where strategy is considered as a plan, a "how," a means of getting from here to there. He further states that strategy can be considered as a perspective, that is, vision and direction. Strategy as the basis for competition is best understood from the perspective of Michael Porter where he states that it means deliberately choosing a different set of activities to deliver a unique mix of value.

LO2 A business model is a conceptual tool that contains a set of elements and their relationships and allows expressing a company's logic of earning money.

It is a description of the value a company offers to one or several segments of customers and the architecture of the firm and its network of partners for creating, marketing and delivering this value and relationship capital, in order to generate profitable and sustainable revenue streams.

LO3 A retail strategy is defined as "a clear and definite plan that the retailer outlines to tap the market and build a long-term relationship with the consumers," A retail strategy is fundamental to the existence of the retail organization/company. It helps define the organization/company, the purpose and how the retailer will face various challenges in the environment and marketplace. The retailer then determines tactics. The strategy document for the retailer thus acts as the guide for how processes, systems and information are handled in the organization/company.

The steps involved in the strategic planning process are (1) Define the mission (2) Analyze the situation (3) Identify options (4) Set objectives (5) Obtain and allocate resources (6) Develop and implement the plan. The results of the plan are evaluated and they serve as a basis for analyzing the situation for the subsequent plans.

An identification of the organization/company's mission and purpose is the starting point of the planning exercise. The mission statement defines what the firm intends to do and how it plans to do it. The plan for achieving these objectives as per the mission statement is based on the analysis of the strengths, weaknesses, opportunities and threats that the firm may face. This is known as the situation analysis. This analysis helps the management identify the various alternatives available to them these include market penetration, format development, market development and diversification.

LO 4 As the retailer grows from the position of one shop to a chain of retail stores and from a local to a regional and national presence, strategy and planning become important. In order to win in retail a retailer needs to have a clear focus and strategy. Michael Porter has identified various elements, which go into the composition of a typical value chain. These include inbound logistics, operations, outbound logistics, marketing and sales, service, procurement, technology development and human resource management.

KEY TERMS
1. Customer intimacy
2. Business mode
3. Competitive strategy
4. Operational excellence
5. Product leadership
6. Industry/sector clock speed
7. Situation analysis
8. Market penetration
9. Mission statement
10. Retail format development
11. Market expansion/
12. development
13. Organic growth
14. Value chain

Review questions

1 What is 'strategy'? Discuss the strategic planning process.

Ans- Increased competition and the expansion of retail markets have forced many retailers to rethink their strategies. Various definitions of strategy prevail and according to Henry Mintzberg people use "strategy" in several different ways, the most common being the one where strategy is considered as a plan, a "how," a means of getting from here to there. He further states that strategy can be considered as a perspective, that is, vision and direction. Strategy as the basis for competition is best understood from the perspective of Michael Porter where he states that it means deliberately choosing a different set of activities to deliver a unique mix of value.

2 What is a business model?

Ans- A business model is a conceptual tool that contains a set of elements and their relationships and allows expressing a company's logic of earning money.
It is a description of the value a company offers to one or several segments of customers and the architecture of the firm and its network of partners for creating, marketing and delivering this value and relationship capital, in order to generate profitable and sustainable revenue streams.

3. Discuss the strategy planning process in retail.

Ans- The steps involved in the strategic planning process are (1) Define the mission (2) Analyze the situation (3) Identify options (4) Set objectives (5) Obtain and allocate resources (6) Develop and implement the plan. The results of the plan are evaluated and they serve as a basis for analyzing the situation for the subsequent plans.

4. How can strategic planning help build a competitive advantage?

Ans- A retail strategy is defined as "a clear and definite plan that the retailer outlines to tap the market and build a long-term relationship with the consumers," A retail strategy is fundamental to the existence of the retail organization/company. It helps define the organization/company, the purpose and how the retailer will face various challenges in the environment and marketplace. The retailer then determines tactics.

The strategy document for the retailer thus acts as the guide for how processes, systems and information are handled in the organization/company.

An identification of the organization/company's mission and purpose is the starting point of the planning exercise. The mission statement defines what the firm intends to do and how it plans to do it. The plan for achieving these objectives as per the mission statement is based on the analysis of the strengths, weaknesses, opportunities and threats that the firm may face. This is known as the situation analysis. This analysis helps the management identify the various alternatives available to them these include market penetration, format development, market development and diversification.

5. Explain the linkages with the elements of the retail value chain.

Ans- As the retailer grows from the position of one shop to a chain of retail stores and from a local to a regional and national presence, strategy and planning become important. In order to win in retail a retailer needs to have a clear focus and strategy. Michael Porter has identified various elements, which go into the composition of a typical value chain. These include inbound logistics, operations, outbound logistics, marketing and sales, service, procurement, technology development and human resource management.

CHAPTER-7 - STORE SITE SELECTION

SUMMARY

LO 1 The location of a retail store continues to occupy an important place m retail strategy. It not only conveys the image of the store, but also influences the merchandise mix and the interior layout of the store. While the merchandise mix can be changed and prices adjusted it is difficult to change the decision on store location very easily.

LO 2,3 A store may be located as a freestanding/isolated store, as a part of a business district or can be a part of a shopping centre. While choosing a retail location a retailer needs to first identify the market that is suitable for his range of products, He then needs to evaluate the market potential and identify the most attractive sites for the store. Depending on the criteria important to the retailer he then takes a decision on the location of the retail store.

LO4 The Indian retail market is developing rapidly. Nearly 25,000,000 sq.ft. of organized retail space is expected to come up by the year 2005. While the market appears to be booming there are some peculiarities that need to be understood. Simple application of Western retail formats and models may not really be relevant in the Indian context.

KEY TERMS
1. Freestanding /Isolated store
2. Shopping center
3. Market potential
4. Geographic information systems
5. Index of retail saturation
6. Central place theory
7. Business district
8. Market identification
9. Trade/exchange area analysis
10. Herfindahl-herschman index
11. Reilly's law of retail Gravitation
12. Huff's model of trading area analysis

Review questions

1. What are the factors that a retailer needs to take into account while choosing a location for a retail store ?

Ans- The location of a retail store continues to occupy an important place m retail strategy. It not only conveys the image of the store, but also influences the merchandise mix and the interior layout of the store. While the merchandise mix can be changed and prices adjusted it is difficult to change the decision on store location very easily.

2. How do facilities like adequate parking and easy access to public transportation affect the developments of shopping areas?

Ans- A store may be located as a freestanding/isolated store, as a part of a business district or can be a part of a shopping centre. While choosing a retail location a retailer needs to first identify the market that is suitable for his range of products. He then needs to evaluate the market potential and identify the most attractive sites for the store. Depending on the criteria important to the retailer he then takes a decision on the location of the retail store.

3. What is a trade/exchange area? Would a trading are vary for different types of retailers? Discuss

Ans- For a retail store, the retail trade/exchange area is the sphere of influence. Determining the trade/exchange area is data-driven because retailers can use transaction data. Yes they would vary for different types of retailers they are in the following:

Itinerant Retailers

These are retailers who do not have a fixed decided place of business. Their business is characterized by moving their shops around, sometimes even on a daily basis. Their sale is to the final consumers of the goods, so they are retailers, even if they do not have a standard place of business.

Fixed Shop Retailers

These are self-explanatory, they operate out of a fixed place of business. They are permanent establishments that do not change their locations very often in search of greener pastures.

Types of Fixed Shop Retailers

1] General Stores: These are the most common stores we find in India. They carry all items of daily use a customer needs from biscuits and grains to toothpaste and shampoos. They are centrally and conveniently located in a local market or a residential area, where they are accessible to the customers.

2] Specialty Stores: These are stores that specifically sell only one line of products, like women wear, electronics, cosmetics etc. They specialize in selling only a variety of products of that one category. Like for example Vijay Sales only sells electronics.

3] Secondhand Goods Store: As the name suggests they sell used goods. These used goods can range from old and rare books to furniture to cars even. They source their products differently than normal retailers, but since the goods are going to final consumers it is still considered a retail trade/exchange.

4] Street Stallholders: These retailers operate out of stalls set up on the street, but their establishments are permanent still. They do not shift their stalls on a regular basis. The stalls are often located in central locations with heavy foot traffic.

4. Discuss the impact of high real estate costs and the general unavailability of large sites in metropolitan areas on the retail industry/sector in India.

Ans The Indian retail market is developing rapidly. Nearly 25,000,000 sq.ft. of organized retail space is expected to come up by the year 2005. While the market appears to be booming there are some peculiarities that need to be understood. Simple application of Western retail formats and models may not really be relevant in the Indian context.

CHAPTER -8 - METHODS OF RETAIL EXPANSION

SUMMARY

LO 1 Retailers have for long looked outside the geographical boundaries of their own countries for enhancing their business. A key element influencing the regions where a firm expands depends on the choice of regions and countries that it has. This is largely governed by the investment climate m the host country/nation and in many cases the allowing of Foreign Direct Investment has played an important role in globalization. In the Indian context 'FDI' means investment by non-resident entity /person resident outside India in the capital of the Indian company. It is thus a method of allowing external finance into an economy. FDI also facilitates international trade/exchange and transfer of knowledge, skills and technology

LO2 There are primarily two routes through which a foreign direct investment is possible in India which are the **Automatic route or Prior Government Approval route**. Over the past few years, India has emerged as a key destination for FDI According to the FDI Confidence Index 2010 released by A T Kearney, India ranks third, in FDI attractiveness ranking.

LO 3, 4, 5 Franchising has evolved from the traditional forms and today touches almost all industries from automobiles to financial services. As a method of retail expansion, franchising has helped retailers like McDonald's and SubWay create an international presence in a very short span of time. Franchising is not a business or an industry/sector, but it is a method used by businesses for the marketing and distribution of their products or services. The two parties, which emerge, are:
*The Franchisor and
* The Franchisee
Franchising represents a great way to develop a national brand. There are four critical success factors that, when combined, can help create a powerful national brand: investment in the franchise infrastructure, an unwavering focus on franchisee economics, aggressive unit growth, and increased scale. Functions such as training, franchise sales, marketing, new product development, public relations, real estate and technology are all crucial. An investment in a fully developed franchise system requires a long-term view.

LO 6, 7 Various theories of retail development explain the process of retail development and revolve around the importance of competitive pressures, the investments in organization/companyal capabilities and the creation of a sustainable competitive advantage.

While many retailers have ventured into the arena of international areas, not many have been successful. Some of the reasons that can be traced to the failure can stem from a basic flawed strategy. While entering a foreign market, a strategy must be based on a complete understanding of the consumers in the market of entry. The retailer must also gauge whether the consumers in that market are in need of the product that the retailer is offering and can relate to the value proposition being offered. Expansion to a new country/nation cannot entail merely taking a proven retail model and exporting it to a new country/nation, where one has to deal with a new set of competitors, a different language and culture, and unique shopper expectations.

KEY TERMS

1. Retail
2. Marketing
3. Consumerism
4. Foreign direct investment
5. Franchise
6. Franchisor
7. Franchisee
8. Business format
9. Product/Trade/exchange name
10. franchising
11. Regional franchise
12. franchising
13. Single unit franchise
14. Master franchise
15. International retail
16. Cautious internationalists
17. Emboldened intemationalists

18. World/global powers
19. Eclectic paradigm
20. Transnational's
21. Multinationals
22. Joint ventures
23. Acquisition
24. Organic growth
25. Aggressive internationalists

Review questions

1. What do you understand by the term Foreign Direct Investment in the Indian context?

Ans- Retailers have for long looked outside the geographical boundaries of their own countries for enhancing their business. A key element influencing the regions where a firm expands depends on the choice of regions and countries that it has. This is largely governed by the investment climate m the host country/nation and in many cases the allowing of Foreign Direct Investment has played an important role in globalization. In the Indian context 'FDI' means investment by non-resident entity /person resident outside India in the capital of the Indian company. It is thus a method of allowing external finance into an economy. FDI also facilitates international trade/exchange and transfer of knowledge, skills and technology

2 Discuss the pros and cons of permitting FDI in Indian retail.

Ans- There are primarily two routes through which a foreign direct investment is possible in India which are the **Automatic route or Prior Government Approval route**. Over the past few years, India has emerged as a key destination for FDI According to the FDI Confidence Index 2010 released by A T Kearney, India ranks third, in FDI attractiveness ranking.

3. Discuss the reasons for the success of franchising as a retail model.

Ans- Franchising has evolved from the traditional forms and today touches almost all industries from automobiles to financial services. As a method of retail expansion, franchising has helped retailers like McDonald's and SubWay create an international presence in a very short span of time. Franchising is not a business or an industry/sector, but it is a method used by businesses for the marketing and distribution of their products or services. The two parties, which emerge, are:

*The Franchisor and

* The Franchisee

Franchising represents a great way to develop a national brand. There are four critical success factors that, when combined, can help create a powerful national brand: investment in the franchise infrastructure, an unwavering focus on franchisee economics, aggressive unit growth, and increased scale. Functions such as training, franchise sales, marketing, new product development, public relations, real estate and technology are all crucial. An investment in a fully developed franchise system requires a long-term view.

4. Explain the concept of international retail and analyze the reasons why retailers to go international

Ans Various theories of retail development explain the process of retail development and revolve around the importance of competitive pressures, the investments in organization/companyal capabilities and the creation of a sustainable competitive advantage.

While many retailers have ventured into the arena of international areas, not many have been successful. Some of the reasons that can be traced to the failure can stem from a basic flawed strategy. While entering a foreign market, a strategy must be based on a complete understanding of the consumers in the market of entry. The retailer must also gauge whether the consumers in that market are in need of the product that the retailer is offering and can relate to the value proposition being offered. Expansion to a new country/nation cannot entail merely taking a proven retail model and exporting it to a new country/nation, where one has to deal with a new set of competitors, a different language and culture, and unique shopper expectations.

5. Why is failure in the arena of international retail common?

Ans- While many retailers have ventured into the arena of international areas, not many have been successful. Some of the reasons that can be traced to the failure can stem from a basic flawed strategy. While entering a foreign market, a strategy must be based on a complete understanding of the consumers in the market of entry. The retailer must also gauge whether the consumers in that market are in need of the product that the retailer is offering and can relate to the value proposition being offered. Expansion to a new country/nation cannot entail merely taking a proven retail model and exporting it to a new country/nation, where one has to deal with a new set of competitors, a different language and culture, and unique shopper expectations.

CHAPTER-9 - BASIS OF RETAIL MERCHANDISING

SUMMARY

LO1 Leading retailers have embraced a seamless blend of art and science that creates a competitive advantage. With the growth of organized retail, the world/global this function has gained in significance. The size of the organization/company, the merchandise to be carried, the types of stores and the organization/company structure affect the merchandising function

LO2 The two key players in this function are the buyer and the merchandiser. There are rarely any two stores organized in the same way, hence, the function of buying and merchandising will also vary from one organization/company to another. The needs of an independent retailer will vary considerably from those of a large chain store operation. In case of a chain store, the buying function may be centralized or decentralized geographically depending on the retail organization/company.

The merchandise to be carried by a retailer largely determines the responsibilities of the merchandiser. The merchandise philosophy is a reflection of the retailers target market that is the customer segment that wishes to cater to. It is keeping this target market in mind that the retailer has to evolve a strategy for store location, pricing and the product assortment that he is going to offer to the customer.

LO 3 The function of buying and merchandising varies from organization/company to organization/company. The role of the buyer and merchandiser would hence vary. Similarly the levels within the hierarchy would also vary. Many a time, the job of a buyer is likened to that of a product manager in a consumer company. Larger retailers provide more sophisticated merchandise information systems that allow quick and efficient responses to changes in the market. They also have established planning processes for seasonal planning, forecasting and assortment planning.

LO 4 In small independent stores one person is typically the owner and the manager. He is responsible for all the business operations of the store, including all the buying and merchandising duties. It is hence necessary that he must have a thorough understanding of the buying process. As the owner has direct access to the end consumers, he would have a better understanding of their needs and wants and the function of buying would be as per the requirements. On the other hand the nerds of the buyer for a chain of stores and a non-store retailer would be very different.

LO 5 The field of merchandising has evolved over the years in keeping with the changes occurring in retail. Products have also evolved to suit the lifestyles of the customer. When a retailer provides merchandise or knowingly adopts a merchandise strategy, which will serve the needs of a specific target audience in keeping with the lifestyles they lead, it is termed as lifestyle merchandising.

LO 6 Multi channel retailing is a reality today. As customers move access channels to make a buying decision retailer need to incorporate the requirements of merchandise across various channel in their merchandise plan.

LO 7 The principles of merchandising are derived from the seven rights of merchandising. They include understanding the target market, building the merchandise plan, one store at a time and creating merchandise as may be required by the customers. Building the right merchandise and offering the right assortment, which is consistent across merchandise lines in the store and offers value is also important. One also needs to keep the needs of the vendor in mind and share information to enable a win. Lastly it is necessary to accept that mistakes happen, however to learn from the same and to continually seek to surprise the customer.

KEY TERMS
1. **Merchandising**
2. **Merchandise analysis**
3. **Merchandise planning**
4. **Merchandiser**
5. **Planner**
6. **Retail buyer**
7. **Merchandise philosophy**
8. **Lifestyle merchandising**

Review questions

1. What is the importance of the function of merchandising in a retail organization/company?

Ans- Leading retailers have embraced a seamless blend of art and science that creates a competitive advantage. With the growth of organized retail the world/global this function has gained in significance. The size of the organization/company, the merchandise to be carried, the types of stores and the organization/company structure affect the merchandising function.

2. What are the factors that affect the function of merchandising in retail?

Ans- The two key players in this function are the buyer and the merchandiser. There are rarely any two stores organized in the same way, hence, the function of buying and merchandising will also vary from one organization/company to another. The needs of an independent retailer will vary considerably from those of a large chain store operation. In case of a chain store, the buying function may be centralized or decentralized geographically depending on the retail organization/company.

The merchandise to be carried by a retailer largely determines the responsibilities of the merchandiser. The merchandise philosophy is a reflection of the retailer's target market that is the customer segment that wishes to cater to. It is keeping this target market in mind that the retailer has to evolve a strategy for store location, pricing and the product assortment that he is going to offer to the customer.

3. Explain the difference between the role of a buyer and the merchandiser. How has this role evolved over the past ten years?

Ans- The function of buying and merchandising varies from organization/company to organization/company. The role of the buyer and merchandiser would hence vary. Similarly, the levels within the hierarchy would also vary. Many a time, the job of a buyer is likened to that of a product manager in a consumer company. Larger retailers provide more sophisticated merchandise information systems that allow quick and efficient responses to changes in the market. They also have established planning processes for seasonal planning, forecasting and assortment planning.

4. How does the function of buying and merchandising vary depending on the size and type of organization/company?

Ans- In small independent stores one person is typically the owner and the manager. He is responsible for all the business operations of the store, including all the buying and merchandising duties. It is hence necessary that he must have a thorough understanding of the buying process. As the owner has direct access to the end consumers, he would have a better understanding of their needs and wants and the function of buying would be as per the requirements. On the other hand the nerds of the buyer for a chain of stores and a non-store retailer would be very different.

5. Explain the concept of lifestyle merchandising. Is this concept applicable in India?

Ans The field of merchandising has evolved over the years in keeping with the changes occurring in retail. Products have also evolved to suit the lifestyles of the customer. When a retailer provides merchandise or knowingly adopts a merchandise strategy, which will serve the needs of a specific target audience in keeping with the lifestyles they lead, it is termed as lifestyle merchandising.

6. What are the principles of merchandising?

Ans- The principles of merchandising are derived from the seven rights of merchandising. They include understanding the target market, building the merchandise plan, one store at a time and creating merchandise as may be required by the customers. Building the right merchandise and offering the right assortment, which is consistent across merchandise lines in the store and offers value is also important. One also needs to keep the needs of the vendor in mind and share information to enable a win. Lastly it is necessary to accept that mistakes happen, however to learn from the same and to continually seek to surprise the customer.

CHAPTER-10 - THE PROCESS OF MERCHANDISE PLANNING

SUMMARY

LO 1 The concept of merchandise planning varies from retailer to retailer. The process of planning starts with the sales forecast. It then moves to calculate the quantities that need to be purchased in various products. The entire process of merchandise planning helps the buyer arrive at the quantities of the produce that need to be bought and has implications on other departments like finance marketing, warehousing, logistics and store operations.

LO 2, LO 3 The merchandising strategy determines the products that would have to be made available, their characteristics and prices. The definition of the value proposition helps in clearly defining the target customer and store positioning, the mix of the products on the basis of the target customer, winch then helps the buyer understand the business model that is adopted by the retailer. The business model helps determine the focus of the retailer.

The next stage is the creation of the merchandise budget, which takes in to consideration the sales that are to be achieved, the inventory levels needed to achieve these sales, the reductions in price that may need to be done, the margins that will be earned and the subsequent purchase levels that will be required. Understanding the merchandise hierarchy helps the buyer determine the levels which planning is required.

The process of merchandise planning may be top down or bottom up. Top down planning occurs when the corporate objectives dictate the company's financial objectives in terms of sales, profit and working capital. The growth and merchandise strategies are then determined on this basis. Bottom up planning on the other hand takes into consideration the various types of stores existing, the space available in them to sell various types of products, what are the options that will be needed and then arrive at the numbers that are needed.

LO 4 In the day of rapid computerization, a large number of retailers use different types of softwares for the purpose of merchandise planning. The tools used may range from simple excel sheets, to specialized softwares like retail Pro JDA, etc.

KEY TERMS

1. Six-month merchandise plan
2. Planned purchases
3. Planned markdowns
4. End-of-Month (EOM) inventory
5. Stock-to-Sales method
6. Percentage variation method
7. Assortment planning
8. Model stock plan
9. Sales forecast
10. Planned sales
11. Planned reductions
12. Planned markup
13. Beginning-of-Month (BOM) inventory
14. Basic stock method
15. Open to buy
16. Range plan

Review questions

1. Explain the importance of merchandise planning in merchandise management.

Ans- The concept of merchandise planning varies from retailer to retailer. The process of planning starts with the sales forecast. It then moves to calculate the quantities that need to be purchased in various products.

2. How would the function of merchandising differ for a lifestyle retailer as compared to a food and grocery retailer?

Ans- The entire process of merchandise planning helps the buyer arrive at the quantities of the produce that need to be bought and has implications on other departments like finance marketing, warehousing, logistics and store operations.

The merchandising strategy determines the products that would have to be made available, their characteristics and prices. The definition of the value proposition helps in clearly defining the target customer and store positioning, the mix of the products on the basis of the target customer, winch then helps the buyer understand the business model that is adopted by the retailer. The business model helps determine the focus of the retailer.

3. What are the elements of merchandise planning?

Ans- Elements of merchandise planning

(1) Product:

Product or merchandise is the basic component of marketing mix. Retailer has to cater to the products that are expected by his segments. He has to maintain adequate inventory of product category expected by his customer.

(2) Price:

Another important component of marketing mix. Price is an important variable in a country/nation like India, where people are price sensitive. Retailer has to determine his segment and the price range to which they belong. Broadly it can be classified as low, Medium and premium range.

(3) Range:

Range refers to width, breadth and depth of products offered for sale. Customers should have opportunity to make choice or selection depending on the type of retail store.

(4) Assortment:
It refer to combination of products made available to customer at retail outlet. Merchandise is assorted and presented category wise and department wise.
E.g. – Cosmetics, Toiletries, Electronics, Staples, Vegetable, Furniture etc., each category further will have different products or different brands at different size and price level.

(5) Space:
Products should visible to visiting customer. Retailer have limited floor space, he should provide adequate space for display of each product. Available space for display of each product is utilized to showcase and presents goods, through different types of fixtures, hangers, gondolas, mannequins, fridge depending on the nature, size, and dimension of goods.

4. What is assortment planning and how does it differ from range planning?
Ans- **Assortment planning** is the process of selecting the collection of products which will be on offer in particular areas (localization) and during specified periods of time (seasonality).
Range planning, from setting the concept, purpose and direction through to selecting the products and finalizing the price, distribution and sales forecast, is a truly iterative process that typically involves buying and merchandising working hand in hand, often with somewhat opposing objectives.

5. Why is assortment planning needed?
Ans- You **need** to use **assortment planning** to get the right buy quantities for each item based on what your customers want. With **assortment planning**, you can make informed decisions about which locations can sell certain items before you buy.

CHAPTER-11 - METHODS OF MERCHANDISE PROCUREMENT

SUMMARY

LO 1 2 Determining the source who would supply the products as required by the retailer in the quantities needed by the retailer, as per the requirements of retailers is an integral part of the buyer's function. To understand the process of sourcing at the retail end, one needs to understand what retailers do and, in particular, how they obtain the merchandise they sell. The function of sourcing enables the buyer to identify, develop and manage resources for manufacturing and supply of products for the retailer.

LO 2 Often retailers use the services of a Resident Buying Office, when sourcing from international markets. The Resident Buying office represents many retailers in the same line of business in the central wholesale market providing information about market developments and guidance in purchasing and actual placing of some orders for their clients. The growth of retail chains and the need to source merchandise at a competitive rate largely fuelled the growth of the resident buying offices. Buying offices may are classified as independently owned offices, Co-operatively Owned Office or an individually owned office. Merchandise brokers and commission offices may also serve the retailers in sourcing merchandise.

LO 3 The term 'sourcing' or 'procurements' means finding or seeking out products from different places, manufactures or suppliers. Sourcing enables the retailer to have winning products.

LO4 The process of sourcing for any item would typically involve:
*Identifying sources of supply
*Contacting the sources of supply
*Evaluating the sources of supply
*Establishing vendor relations and
*Analyzing vendor performance

The first step in the process of sourcing is to identify the sources of supply. It needs to be decided at this time whether the product will be sourced from the domestic market or from the international market. Contacting a source of supply may be as simple as having a representative visit the office and meet with the buyer and showcase a collection of the merchandise. This is often termed as a vendor-initiated contact.

Once the sources of supply are identified they need to be evaluated. The evaluation criteria would vary from retailer to retailer. Stage four of this process involves active negotiations with the vendors. The aim of the function of sourcing is the optimization of costs through optimization of vendor performance. It is necessary that the needs and the requirements of the retail organization/company are synchronized with the abilities and the aims of the supplier. Vendor performance has far reaching impact on the value and the cost incurred by the retailer and eventually affects retailer performance.

KEY TERMS
1. Sourcing
2. International sources of supply
3. Domestic sources
4. Quantity discount
5. Central marketplace
6. Trade/exchange discounts
7. Cash discount
8. Seasonal discount
9. Gross margin contribution
10. Global sourcing
11. The Resident buying office

Review Questions

1. Explain the importance of sourcing in the merchandise process.

Ans- Determining the source who would supply the products as required by the retailer in the quantities needed by the retailer, as per the requirements of retailers is an integral part of the buyer's function. To understand the process of sourcing at the retail end, one needs to understand what retailers do and, in particular, how they obtain the merchandise they sell. The function of sourcing enables the buyer to identify, develop and manage resources for manufacturing and supply of products for the retailer.

2 What are the factors affecting the sources of supply?

Ans - Some of the more important **factors affecting supply** are the good's own price, the prices of related goods, production costs, technology, the production function, and expectations of sellers.

3. What are the key factors affecting vendor negotiations?

Ans-Factors affecting vendor negotiations:

(i) The goals and interests of the parties

(ii) The extent to which the negotiating parties are interdependent

(iii) The past relations which exist between the two negotiating parties

(iv) The nature, temperament, and personalities of the parties

(v) The persuasive ability of each party

4. What are the legal issues involved in sourcing of merchandise from domestic and international markets?

Ans- The term 'sourcing' or 'procurements' means finding or seeking out products from different places, manufactures or suppliers. Sourcing enables the retailer to have winning products.

5 Briefly explain each of the following terms:
(a) Resident buying office
(b) Resident buyer
(c) Independent buying office
(d) Salaried or fixed fee office
(e) Commission or merchandise-broker office

Answers

Often retailers use the services of a Resident Buying Office, when sourcing from international markets. The Resident Buying office represents many retailers in the same line of business in the central wholesale market providing information about market developments and guidance in purchasing and actual placing of some orders for their clients. The growth of retail chains and the need to source merchandise at a competitive rate largely fuelled the growth of the resident buying offices. Buying offices may are classified as independently owned offices, Co-operatively Owned Office or an individually owned office. Merchandise brokers and commission offices may also serve the retailers in sourcing merchandise.

CHAPTER-12 - RETAIL PRICING AND EVALUATING MERCHANDISE PERFORMANCE

SUMMARY

LO 1 Arriving at the right price for a product or service is one of the most difficult tasks of marketing. In order to arrive at the retail price, one needs to first consider the elements that go into the making of the price. The elements to be considered are the cost of goods, and the merchandise margins.

Various other factors like the target market, store policies, competition and the economic conditions need to be taken into consideration while arriving at the price of a product. The pricing strategy adopted by a retailer may be cost-oriented pricing, demand-oriented pricing or competition-oriented pricing.

LO 2 In order to arrive at the retail price, the first element that needs to be considered is the Cost of Goods, and the various other expenses, which are involved in the movement of the goods from the manufacturer to the actual store. These expenses may be Fixed or Variable. The cost of a product is the total of the fixed and variable expenses to manufacturer or offers your product or service. Price on the other hand is the selling price per unit customers pay for your product or service

LO 3,4 The pricing strategies that may be followed include, Market skimming, Market Penetration, Leader pricing, Price bundling, Multi-unit pricing, Discount pricing, Everyday low pricing and Odd pricing. Adjustments to retail prices are made by way of markdowns. Markdowns are a permanent reduction in price and may be taken as a result of slow selling or as part of a systematic strategy.

LO 5 Most retailers classify their stores as A, B, or C based on their sales potential. Each chain's allocation of merchandise to stores is different, but it should be based on the total number of stores in the chain and the distribution of sales among stores. Each store, regardless of size, must carry a large proportion of the assortment offered; otherwise the customers will perceive the smaller stores as having an inferior assortment

LO 6 Merchandise performance can be evaluated by using ABC analysis, a sell through analysis or by the multiple attribute method. The Gross Margin Return on investment of GMROI is a useful tool for merchandise planning. It can help identify products, which are winners and those that need attention. Other methods of managing inventory investments include predetermining the reorder point and by determining the Economic Order Quantity.

KEY TERMS

1. Fixed cost
2. Cumulative markup
3. Markup
4. Market skimming
5. Leader pricing
6. Odd pricing
7. Markdown
8. Variable cost
9. Initial markup
10. Price
11. Market penetration
12. Multi-unit pricing
13. Single pricing
14. GMROI
15. Break-even revenue
16. Maintained markup
17. Price range
18. Price bundling
19. Every day bow pricing
20. Multiple pricing

Review Questions

1. What is meant by 'retail price? What are the factors affecting retail pricing?

Ans- Arriving at the right price for a product or service is one of the most difficult tasks of marketing. In order to arrive at the retail price, one needs to first consider the elements that go into the making of the price. The elements to be considered are the cost of goods, and the merchandise margins. Various other factors like the target market, store policies, competition and the economic conditions need to be taken into consideration while arriving at the price of a product. The pricing strategy adopted by a retailer may be cost-oriented pricing, demand-oriented pricing or competition-oriented pricing.

2 Explain the elements of retail price.

Ans- In order to arrive at the retail price, the first element that needs to be considered is the Cost of Goods, and the various other expenses, which are involved in the movement of the goods from the manufacturer to the actual store. These expenses may be Fixed or Variable. The cost of a product is the total of the fixed and variable expenses to manufacturer or offers your product or service. Price on the other hand is the selling price per unit customers pay for your product or service.

3. Can stores apply uniform markups on all the products that they buy?

Ans- The pricing strategies that may be followed include, Market skimming, Market Penetration, Leader pricing, Price bundling, Multi-unit pricing, Discount pricing, Everyday low pricing and Odd pricing. Adjustments to retail prices are made by way of markdowns. Markdowns are a permanent reduction in price and may be taken as a result of slow selling or as part of a systematic strategy.

4. What are the causes of markdowns?

Ans- Overbuying, duplication, poor timing of deliveries, bad assortment planning, are all recognized causes of markdowns. Excessive markdowns raise the cost of goods sold and result in a reduction in gross margin.

5.Why do some retailers opt for markdowns only at the end of the season?

Ans-Markdowns are inevitable in **retail**. Typically, they come because a poor decision was made when buying. Since buying inventory **is** about math way more than it **is** about your fashion sense.

CHAPTER-13 THE DEVELOPMENT OF PRIVATE LABELS

SUMMARY

LO 1 When the retailer decides to sell products or a line of merchandise which is owned, controlled, merchandised and sold by the retailer in his own store/chain of stores, he is said to be selling own label/brand or private label merchandise. A private label can be classified as either a store brand, an umbrella brand or individual brand.

LO 2 Across the globe, as retailers become more sophisticated and competitive, the role of private label in their store's changes from that of a price-fighter to being a value-added marketing differentiator. This is indicated by the fact that the volume of private-label merchandise has been on the rise in all retail sectors over the past decade. Private label brands are starting to diversify their offering beyond the expected, enabling them to compete more effectively in existing product categories and foray into new and different product categories that have traditionally been dominated by national brand players.

The most significant advantage that a private label allows a retailer is that of earning a level of margin, which may be higher than what is offered on other brands that he chooses to retail. A private label basically involves the retailer doing the designing, merchandising, sourcing and distribution. Thus, his costs are under his control and spread across a limited range of activities.

LO 3 In the developed markets, private labels started out of economic necessity for providing a cheap alternative for low-emotion involvement goods such as butter, eggs, flour, and sugar. Generics, which were products distinguishable by their plain and basic packaging, were the first type of private labels to appear on the horizon largely associated with low price and low quality.

LO 4 Throughout the world/global, the private label is winning acceptability and the loyalty of customers. The process of private label creation is to a great extent similar to the process involved in the sourcing of merchandise. The steps involved in the creation of the private label include defining the objective, understanding and defining the gaps in the market, taking a decision on Make or Buy and sourcing and determining the marketing and sales strategy and the measures of performance.

KEY TERMS
1. Store brand
2. Generies
3. Individual brand
4. Umbrella brand

Review Questions

1. What are private labels? What are the different categories in which they can be classified? Give examples of Indian private labels in each of the categories.

Ans- When the retailer decides to sell products or a line of merchandise which is owned, controlled, merchandised and sold by the retailer in his own store/chain of stores, he is said to be selling own label/brand or private label merchandise. A private label can be classified as either a store brand, an umbrella brand or individual brand.

2. What are the reasons for the emergence of private labels in the world/global of retail?

Ans- Across the globe, as retailers become more sophisticated and competitive, the role of private label in their store's changes from that of a price-fighter to being a value-added marketing differentiator. This is indicated by the fact that the volume of private-label merchandise has been on the rise in all retail sectors over the past decade. Private label brands are starting to diversify their offering beyond the expected, enabling them to compete more effectively in existing product categories and foray into new and different product categories that have traditionally been dominated by national brand players.

The most significant advantage that a private label allows a retailer is that of earning a level of margin, which may be higher than what is offered on other brands that he chooses to retail. A private label basically involves the retailer doing the designing, merchandising, sourcing and distribution. Thus, his costs are under his control and spread across a limited range of activities. In the developed markets, private labels started out of economic necessity for providing a cheap alternative for low-emotion involvement goods such as butter, eggs, flour, and sugar. Generics, which were products distinguishable by their plain and basic packaging, were the first type of private labels to appear on the horizon largely associated with low price and low quality.

3. Explain the process of private label creation.

Ans- Throughout the world/global, the private label is winning acceptability and the loyalty of customers. The process of private label creation is to a great extent similar to the process involved in the sourcing of merchandise. The steps involved in the creation of the private label include defining the objective, understanding and defining the gaps in the market, taking a decision on Make or Buy and sourcing and determining the marketing and sales strategy and the measures of performance.

4. Over a period of the next 5 years, analyze the sectors which are likely to see the emergence of private labels in the country/nation. Explain your answer.

Ans- There is a new retail revolution underway, and it's going to affect the food industry/sector across the globe over the next five years in ways we have never seen before. We're talking about the development of private-label products and the new challenges that this will present for brands and manufacturers across the globe, as retailers develop and market their own products rather multinational name brands to meet changing consumer needs.

Consumers today are connected at all times and have access to endless information. As a result, their expectations are changing and they're shopping differently. Many now see private-label brands as being equivalent to or substitutable for multinational brands. When consumers consider quality, many view private-label products as good and getting better. For example, we see this with the extensions into premium private-label products, where quality is very good. Examples include wine, specialty groceries, coffee, and prepared/ready-to-cook chilled meals of restaurant quality.

CHAPTER-14 - CATERGORY MANAGEMENT

SUMMARY

LO1 The evolution of the concept of category management is closely linked to the developments in the field of supply chain management and technology. Technology plays a key role, as information is a key enabler. The idea is to use this information to tailor the product offering to consumer needs. The offering is then measured in terms of sales, cost and returns per square foot. The whole process is aimed at providing customer satisfaction and at the same time maximizing returns for the organization/company. This focus causes a re-evaluation of many prevalent business practices, which may have obstructed a greater understanding of consumer needs and opportunities.

LO 2 Category management is considered the "new science of retailing" for various reasons. Quite simply category management involves organizing and managing promotions, merchandising and distribution activity around the way consumers view and buy a product. A number of specific industry/sector trends are driving the emergence of category management. The key reasons are consumer changes, economic and efficiency considerations, competitive pressures and information technology advances.

LO3 Category management draws attention to various kinds of unproductive departmental separations by emphasizing that categories should be defined first and foremost by consumer need and not by departmental separations. There are six components, which are key to the functioning of category management. Two of these are considered essential without which category management cannot be started and are therefore called core components, the other four are needed to enable the process, without these category management can be started but not institutionalized on an on-going basis. The two core components are strategy and business processes. The enabling factors are performance measurement, information technology, organization/companyal capabilities and co-operative trading partner relationships.

LO 4 The entire process of category management revolves around the partnership between the supplier and the retailer. The success of the partnership is critical to both. Many retailers follow the method of appointing "category captains" to develop a category and further the partnership.

The full-scale adoption of category management requires a considerable amount of reorganization/company on the part of the retailer. People and not the process or computers drive the category management process.

LO 5 The full-scale adoption of category management requires a considerable amount of reorganization/company within the retailer and involves skill development, supplier partnerships, and dealing with the reluctance to change inappropriate organization/companyal structures; and the lack of clear strategic plans for product ranges. Another concern with the implementation of category management is the resulting lack of variety offered to customers. Concentrating on efficiency in logistics and merchandising may result in highly efficient retailing; however, there is a risk that the consumer experience is being given lower priority. A further drawback of category management is the threat to smaller suppliers.

KEY TERMS
1. Efficient consumer response
2. Category definition
3. Preferred / Routine category
4. Category assessment
5. Traffic building
6. Profit generating
7. Image enhancing
8. Category review
9. Performance measurement
10. Category role
11. Occasional /Seasonal category
12. Category performance measures
13. Transaction building

14. Cash generating
15. Category tactics
16. Category captain
17. Co-operative trading partner relationships
18. Destination category
19. Convenience category
20. Category strategy
21. Turf defending
22. Excitement creating
23. Category plan implementation

Review questions

1. What is 'Category Management'? What are the reasons for its emergence?
Ans- The evolution of the concept of category management is closely linked to the developments in the field of supply chain management and technology. Technology plays a key role, as information is a key enabler. The idea is to use this information to tailor the product offering to consumer needs. The offering is then measured in terms of sales, cost and returns per square foot. The whole process is aimed at providing customer satisfaction and at the same time maximizing returns for the organization/company. This focus causes a re-evaluation of many prevalent business practices, which may have obstructed a greater understanding of consumer needs and opportunities.

Category management is considered the "new science of retailing" for various reasons. Quite simply category management involves organizing and managing promotions, merchandising and distribution activity around the way consumers view and buy a product. A number of specific industry/sector trends are driving the emergence of category management. The key reasons are consumer changes, economic and efficiency considerations, competitive pressures and information technology advances.

2. Explain the Category Management Business Process.

Ans- Category management draws attention to various kinds of unproductive departmental separations by emphasizing that categories should be defined first and foremost by consumer need and not by departmental separations. There are six components, which are key to the functioning of category management. Two of these are considered essential without which category management cannot be started and are therefore called core components, the other four are needed to enable the process, without these category management can be started but not institutionalized on an on-going basis. The two core components are strategy and business processes. The enabling factors are performance measurement, information technology, organization/companyal capabilities and co-operative trading partner relationships.

3. What is the significance of category definition and the identification of category roles?

Ans- In general, category management is the process of bundling like products into a singular category, or business unit, and then addressing procurement, merchandising, sales, and other retail efforts on the category as a whole.

A central idea behind this strategy is to emphasize the benefits of the category for the consumer and remove inefficiencies and unprofitable competition among brands and suppliers within a category. For instance, this approach can help retailers lift profits on similar products in multiple ways, including by organizing procurement efforts under a single category instead of by individual brand or supplier.

Depending on a chain's identity and value proposition, categories vary in importance and in terms of the roles that they play within the chain's portfolio of departments and categories.

As advocated by The Partnering Group (TPG), there are four basic category roles — destination, routine, convenience and occasional/seasonal. The roles establish a category's place within the chain's portfolio and form the basis for the allocation of resources.

The roles distinguish categories in terms of their attractiveness and strategic importance:

Strategic Importance: Is there high synergy between the category and the chain? Is the category well aligned with the chain's purpose and identity? Is it important to target shoppers?

Two measures that help assess the strategic fit with shoppers are chain loyalty and propensity. Another relevant metric is the Fair Share Index:

$$Fair\ Share\ Index\ =\ \frac{Value\ Share\ of\ Chain\ in\ Category}{Value\ Share\ of\ Chain\ in\ All\ categories}$$

The fair share index reflects the importance of the category to the retail chain, in terms of the chain's contribution to category sales.
Category attractiveness: Size and growth rate in terms of volume, value, profitability. Destination categories rank high on strategic fit as well as category attractiveness. They are central to the chain's identity and of strategic importance to their business.

Routine categories rank medium to high on strategic fit and category importance. Their presence and offering also has an important bearing on store selection. They reinforce the banner's identity and image, but not to the same extent as destination categories. Tea and pet foods for example are routine categories at Cold Storage.

Supermarket chains usually stocks a limited range of magazines and newspapers, but usually no books. Some chains however made an exception for the exceedingly popular Harry Potter series, at the time the books were released. This served to excite their younger shoppers, and provided convenience to them and their parents.

Convenience categories such as books and stationery at supermarkets rank low on strategic fit and category importance. Their presence provides for a one-stop shopping convenience for the chain's shoppers.

Seasonal or occasional categories include New Year's greeting cards, Christmas and Chinese New Year goodies, and categories like sun block or insecticides in Europe.

4. Explain the role of the Category Captain

Ans- The entire process of category management revolves around the partnership between the supplier and the retailer. The success of the partnership is critical to both. Many retailers follow the method of appointing "category captains" to develop a category and further the partnership.

The full-scale adoption of category management requires a considerable amount of reorganization/company on the part of the retailer. People and not the process or computers drive the category management process.

5. List the drawbacks of the Category Management Process.

Ans- The full-scale adoption of category management requires a considerable amount of reorganization/company within the retailer and involves skill development, supplier partnerships, and dealing with the reluctance to change inappropriate organization/companyal structures; and the lack of clear strategic plans for product ranges. Another concern with the implementation of category management is the resulting lack of variety offered to customers. Concentrating on efficiency in logistics and merchandising may result in highly efficient retailing; however, there is a risk that the consumer experience is being given lower priority. A further drawback of category management is the threat to smaller suppliers.

CHAPTER-15 - HUMAN RESOURSE MANAGEMENT IN RETAIL- A STRATEGIC TOOL

SUMMARY

LO01 In the new economy, human capital is the foundation of value creation, In most cases it becomes an asset which is the most important but at the same time the least understood and measured. In the case of the retail organization/company the human capital is the asset which very often is the starting point of the interaction between the retailer and the customer.

The early 1990's saw the emergence of Human Resources as a key factor within the gamut of the company's strategy and its implementation. Over the years the function of human resources has evolved to being considered from a strategic perspective. In India, attracting people to the retail industry/sector and then retaining them is a challenge. The primary reason for such a situation is the poor image that the business carries.

LO 2 Human Resource Management or HRM as a concept has been widely accepted in most developed countries. HRM is the process of managing organization/companyal employees in an effective way. To implement the management process, HRM cannot be separated from the HR practices comprising selection and recruitment, training, rewarding, expatriate management, etc. and general HR policies and procedures. Strategic Human Resource Management is the practice of aligning business strategy with that of HR practices to achieve the strategic goals of the organization/company. Strategic HRM begins with the notion that HRM practices are tools managers have at their disposal to achieve organization/companyal goals.

LO 3 The Human Resources function in retail involves, identifying various roles in the organization/company, recruiting the persons with the right attitude to fit the jobs, Training, Motivation of employees, and evaluation of employee performance.

LO 4 In retail, as in any other business, defining the organization/company structure is the starting point for managing a business. The first step in creating an organization/company structure, which will work for the retailer, is to define the various tasks/activities that need to be performed. The purpose of this classification is two fold. It helps the various tasks to be identified and it also helps in understanding the roles to be played by people within the organization/company. Once these tasks have been identified the management needs to take into consideration its own requirements and targets and how they can be achieved.

KEY TERMS

1. 7S Framework
2. Strategic human resource management
3. Training
4. Recruitment
5. Employee performance
6. Motivation
7. Mazur plan

Review questions

1. What are the reasons for the increase in importance of the human resource functions in retail?
Ans- In the new economy, human capital is the foundation of value creation, In most cases it becomes an asset which is the most important but at the same time the least understood and measured. In the case of the retail organization/company the human capital is the asset which very often is the starting point of the interaction between the retailer and the customer.

The early 1990's saw the emergence of Human Resources as a key factor within the gamut of the company's strategy and its implementation. Over the years the function of human resources has evolved to being considered from a strategic perspective. In India, attracting people to the retail industry/sector and then retaining them is a challenge. The primary reason for such a situation is the poor image that the business carries.

2. What employee needs would a retailer consider while determining the benefits package and setting employment terms in metro India?

Ans- The Human Resources function in retail involves, identifying various roles in the organization/company, recruiting the persons with the right attitude to fit the jobs, Training, Motivation of employees, and evaluation of employee performance.

3. What traits and competencies would you look for while hiring management Supervisory and operational staff in different departments?

Ans- 1. Supervising Others

Managing others can be a challenge for the **new supervisor** who has not had management experience. Training new managers on what to do, as well as what not to do, can help to minimize issues related to supervising others. For instance, when an employee is promoted to supervisor and then is put in the position to manage those who were peers, they must learn how to make that sometimes difficult transition. Learning how to navigate this sensitive situation can help the new supervisor be successful.

2. Conflict Resolution

Conflict in the workplace is an inevitable reality. It is important to manage this conflict because unresolved conflict can affect relationships between people and groups of people. Both of which can have a major impact on organization/companyal culture and worker productivity.

3. Emotional Intelligence

Emotional intelligence is defined as "the capacity to be aware of, control, and express one's emotions, and to handle interpersonal relationships judiciously and empathetically."Emotional intelligence (EI) is a skill that can be learned and is a mark of professional maturity.

4. Communication Skills

Managers need to have good written and verbal communication skills to effectively manage employees. Additionally, there needs to be a **structured communication process** to filter information throughout the organization/company.

5. Manage Performance

To effectively manage employees, managers need to understand the basics of **managing performance**.

4. Develop a motivation mechanism for a graduate shop floor salesperson.

Answers-

1. Remember that every person is different
Different people are motivated by different things. Some employees would like to be given a challenge to meet, while others will prefer to feel more support and guidance in their day-to-day tasks. People also care about different things. If an employee is interested in a specific department of your business, let them work there. By allowing them to work in an area they find interesting, you will motivate them, and other team members will notice how much attention you are paying to them.

2. Nurture a recognition-rich culture
Motivation doesn't just come from the top. Having a happy and active workforce helps to create an atmosphere that can keep retail staff going. Nurturing a <u>recognition-rich culture</u> where employees of all levels actively congratulate each other on their successes is important. If you have morning meetings, it can be helpful to highlight areas where individual employees excelled the day before. By openly praising people, you can also facilitate a more agile workforce. When employees are encouraged to highlight each other's successes, they learn to respect each other's strengths, which in turn can encourage retail staff to share the load.

3. Give employees responsibility
Playing to each team member's strengths is one of the best ways to ensure that your team is the best that it can be. Allowing staff to take responsibility for areas of the shop that enthuse them can allow them both the opportunity to grow and the chance to encourage other employees to care about the same area.

4. Create a positive atmosphere
To motivate your staff to sell your product, your retail space has to look its best. Create a space that reflects your brand and the lifestyle you are selling to your customers. This environment will help keep your staff motivated and help them take pride in what they do. A pleasant atmosphere, combined with the right attitude from your employees, will, in turn, help you sell more.

5. Encourage development
It doesn't matter if your business is small and you don't have the option to offer promotions – you can still help your staff develop. Offer them some benefits that will motivate them and encourage them to grow. For example, offer the opportunity to learn how you market your store or the opportunity to run your social media accounts. These types of development opportunities will help them learn new skills, while helping you gain some valuable exposure for your shop.

CHAPTER-16 - RETAIL STORE OPERATIONS

SUMMARY

LO 1 The store is an important aspect of the retail business. Purchase decision and the perception and image of the store are made here. From the managements' point of view, operations of the store are a major element of the cost. As a consequence, the store is a critical asset of the retail business and it is imperative that the operations are managed well to achieve and sustain customer satisfaction and be cost effective

LO 2 The Store Manager has to play a dual role in a retail environment. On one hand he is responsible for the various members of the staff and team who to him and enable the smooth functioning of the day to day operations of the store, On the other hand he also has to ensure that the policies and the guidelines as laid down by the management are adhered to by the store and all the employees within the store. The people-intensive and customer interactive nature of their work means store managers play a critical role in ensuring the store supports the overall mission of the company.

LO 3 Processes, people and tasks need to be defined by the management to ensure the smooth flow of operations.
The 5 s model is a combination of five key elements, of which three elements of space, stock and staff are controllable. The other two elements include systems and standards. Systems refer not only to information technology but also to procedures on how things are done at the retailer. Standards on the other hand refer to the set of guidelines. The model attempts to simplify the complexities of retail operations and can be used as a problem-solving technique by offering a straightforward and noncomplex technique.

LO 4 The primary cause of retail shrinkage is pilferage, which can be stealing, which could be employee theft and/or shoplifting. The other cause of retail shrinkage could also be accounting errors. In order to deter theft from occurring on their premises many retailers install surveillance equipment across the store.

KEY TERMS

1. Store operations
2. Shrinkage Store
3. Store operations manual
4. Store administration
5. Staffing
6. Theft
7. Merchandising

Review questions

1. Examine the criticality of the role of operations in the retailing industry/sector through its various stages of maturity.

Ans- The store is an important aspect of the retail business. Purchase decision and the perception and image of the store are made here. From the managements' point of view, operations of the store are a major element of the cost. As a consequence, the store is a critical asset of the retail business and it is imperative that the operations are managed well to achieve and sustain customer satisfaction and be cost effective.

2. What are the different tasks that need to be performed in a retail store from an operational perspective?

Ans-Retailers need staff in their stores to do a wide variety of tasks: help customers, process POS transactions, handle new shipment arrivals, arrange merchandise and take inventory. Automated algorithmic-based labor scheduling tools can optimize staff at peak hours and ensure they remain at their productive best.

3. What are the key factors to be considered and planned for when there are event and promotions in store?

Ans- Promotions are almost always part of a retailer's sales and marketing mix, and for good reason — they can drive sales and help you move inventory.

Bring about a sense of urgency
Avoid setting promotions with no end date, as this will cause people to dilly-dally. It's best to implement limited-time offers to encourage customers to get a move on. This is one of the reasons why flash sales are so effective. Shoppers know that the promo won't last long, so they act quickly. Studies have shown that 50% of flash sale purchases happen in the first hour.

Have a theme
Create your offers around a specific theme. Doing so will make it easier for people to grasp and remember your promotion. An easy way to do this is to piggyback on holidays. Mother's Day, Memorial Day, Labor Day, and the like can always be used as themes. You should also consider piggybacking on "unofficial" holidays. For example, on National Pound Cake Day, (March 4) BirchboxMan ran a promotion to entice people to "gift" a Birchbox subscription.

Combine promotions
If you're feeling particularly generous (or if you really need to liquidate your stock), consider combining different promotions. Initiatives like "Take an *additional* 20% off *already discounted* items" can really grab shopper attention. If you're selling online, try combining discount or BOGO offers with free shipping and see how your customers respond.

Implement targeted offers
It's best to target your promotions towards specific customer groups. Consider creating customer segments according to gender, age group, or spending habits.

For example, if you want to run a sale for a specific brand or designer, you could create a group consisting of people who purchased that brand in the past, then run a promotion specifically for those customers.

Use a solid retail platform to implement your promotions
Promotions may bring about a large wave of sales, and you need to be able to implement your offers smoothly while tracking your transactions and inventory with ease.

4. What is the role played by the store manager in promoting operational efficiency in a retail store?

Ans- The Store Manager has to play a dual role in a retail environment. On one hand he is responsible for the various members of the staff and team who to him and enable the smooth functioning of the day to day operations of the store, On the other hand he also has to ensure that the policies and the guidelines as laid down by the management are adhered to by the store and all the employees within the store. The people-intensive and customer interactive nature of their work means store managers play a critical role in ensuring the store supports the overall mission of the company.

5. Explain the '5 S' model and its significance to store operations.

Ans- Processes, people and tasks need to be defined by the management to ensure the smooth flow of operations. The 5 s model is a combination of five key elements, of which three elements of space, stock and staff are controllable. The other two elements include systems and standards. Systems refer not only to information technology but also to procedures on how things are done at the retailer. Standards on the other hand refer to the set of guidelines. The model attempts to simplify the complexities of retail operations and can be used as a problem-solving technique by offering a straightforward and non-complex technique.

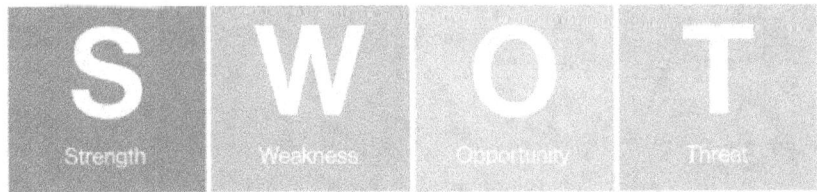

CHAPTER-17 - THE LEGAL AND ETHICAL ASPECTS OF THE RETAIL BUSINESS

SUMMARY

LO 1 Every industry/sector has certain laws which are applicable to it and retail is in no way any different. At the company/retailer level, various legal implications need to be considered. Every organization/company operating in the country/nation needs to consider the legalities involved in direct and indirect taxation. The central government takes care of the tax on income, central excise, service tax, customs tax. The state government levies charges on VAT or sales tax, land revenue, state excise. Local bodies are also empowered to levy taxes on properties, octroi and for utilities like water supply, drainage, etc. Sales tax is a type of indirect tax levied by the government at the point of sale on retail goods and services.

LO 2, 3 The provisions of the law of the land need to be understood and followed by the retailer. Some important laws which the retailer needs to take cognizance of are:
1. Employees' State Insurance Act (ESIC)
2. Payment of Bonus Act
3. Payment of Gratuity Act, 1972
4. Employees Provident Fund Act
5. The Minimum Wages Act, 1948
6. The Employment of Women Act
7. The Shops and Establishments License
8. The Prevention of Food Adulteration (PFA) License
9. The Consumer Protection Act, 1986
10. Essential Commodities Act 1955
11. The Standards of Weights and Measures Act, 1976 and the Standards of Weight and Measures (Packaged Commodities) Rules, 1977

LO 4, 5 The ethical practices of businesses have become an increasingly important issue today. Like in any other business, the bottom line of retail venture is profitability. Retailers need to adhere to the law of the land and the regulations created to monitor business and trade/exchange. World/global over, most industries have also awakened to the implications of environmentalism. This largely is a result of increased public awareness. The melting of the icebergs, changing temperatures in summer and winter and other such natural changes have made consumers aware of the changes happening in their environment and the reasons for the same.

KEY TERMS

1. Sales Tax
2. Value added tax
3. Employees state insurance act, 1948
4. Payment of bonus act, 1985
5. Payment of gratuity act, 1972
6. Employees provident fund Act
7. The employment of women Act
8. The prevention of food adulteration (PFA) license
9. The minimum wages act, 1948
10. The shops and establishments License
11. Bureau of Indian standards
12. Hallmarking
13. The consumer protection act, 1986
14. Agmark
15. Ethics in retail
16. Green retail

Review questions

1. List out the various legal factors that a retailer has to bear in mind before setting up a retail store an India

Ans-Factors:

Retail Store Location and Site Selection

One of the key starting points in putting up a retail store is the right location. Getting into an ideal business location is a sustainable advantage since a competitor can't copy or steal your spot. The challenge is deciding what location is ideal.

Factors influencing in the location of a new retail outlet include the amount of passing foot traffic and local parking availability, as well as rent costs. If you plan to sell a large assortment of goods, a standalone store in a high-traffic business district might make sense. With a more niche store or boutique, a premier spot in an enclosed mall or strip plaza often makes more since you rely on passers-by. Building cost or lease fees play a role as you want to find the best value possible.

Target Market

The ideal location is also one that is close to your target market. You should assess the local marketplace before signing a building contract. If you operate a niche shop, the size and traits of the local marketplace play a key role. If you don't have enough customers that match your target market characteristics, your business model won't work. If you invest in a larger discount or department store, you have to pull customers from a broader geographic area to make enough revenue and profit. This factor influences how much you need to invest in marketing.

Competitive Factors

Competitive factors also impact effectiveness of a retail start-up. The ideal scenario exists when you start a distinct business that offers a sizable marketplace goods or services they value and can't get elsewhere. In general, starting a business in a market with little to no competition is idea. However, the lack of competition may result from barriers to entry, lack of market demand or failed attempts by previous players. Management learning website <u>Mind Tools</u> suggests that you conduct a SWOT analysis to see whether your current strengths and weaknesses, combined with future opportunities and threats, give you a good competitive position.

Financial Capital

You have two basic ways to start a retail business. You can build one from scratch or invest in a franchise, where you purchase the rights to an existing model. In either case, you need some financial capital to start. If you don't have enough savings on your own, you can raise money from investors or lenders, though they must recognize the viability of your business plan. Along with start-up money to open the doors, you need enough capital to buy inventory and to comfortably sustain operations while you work to achieve profit.

Legal and Regulatory Environment

You also need to understand legal and regulatory facts that impact your industry/sector. Some industries are heavily regulated, while others have minimal government regulations. **PESTLE** Analysis recommends that you run a PESTLE exercise to figure out the political, economic, social, legal and environmental factors that might impact the viability of your business. Loose regulations make it easier to open up shop. However, you may need to get professional or business licenses in some cases. To sell insurance, for instance, you need various licenses. If you want to open a pet shop, you need to understand federal and local laws on proper care and sale of animals.

2. What is the government's policy towards Foreign Direct investment in retail in India?

Ans- Every industry/sector /sector has certain laws which are applicable to it and retail is in no way any different. At the company/retailer level, various legal implications need to be considered. Every organization/company operating in the country/nation needs to consider the legalities involved in direct and indirect taxation. The central government takes care of the tax on income, central excise, service tax, customs tax. The state government levies charges on VAT or sales tax, land revenue, state excise. Local bodies are also empowered to levy taxes on properties, octroi and for utilities like water supply, drainage, etc. Sales tax is a type of indirect tax levied by the government at the point of sale on retail goods and services.

3. Explain the significance of the Competition Act in the context of Indian retail.

Ans- The Competition Act, 2002 was enacted by the Parliament of India and governs Indian competition law. It replaced the archaic The Monopolies and Restrictive Trade/exchange Practices Act, 1969. Under this legislation, the Competition Commission of India was established to prevent the activities that have an adverse effect on competition in India. This act extends to whole of India.

It is a tool to implement and enforce competition policy and to prevent and punish anti-competitive business practices by firms and unnecessary Government interference in the market. Competition laws is equally applicable on written as well as oral agreement, arrangements between the enterprises or persons.

The Competition Act, 2002 was amended by the Competition (Amendment) Act, 2007 and again by the Competition (Amendment) Act, 2009. The Act establishes a Commission which is duty bound to protect the interests of free and fair competition (including the process of competition), and as a consequence, protect the interests of consumers. Broadly, the Commission's duty is:-

- To prohibit the agreements or practices that have or are likely to have an appreciable adverse effect on competition in a market in India, (horizontal and vertical agreements / conduct);
- To prohibit the abuse of dominance in a market;
- To prohibit acquisitions, mergers, amalgamations etc. between enterprises which have or are likely to have an appreciable adverse effect on competition in market(s) in India.

In addition to this, the Competition Act envisages its enforcement with the aid of mutual international support and enforcement network across the world/global.

4. What are the ethical dilemmas that a retailer faces?

Ans- The ethical practices of businesses have become an increasingly important issue today. Like in any other business, the bottom line of retail venture is profitability. Retailers need to adhere to the law of the land and the regulations created to monitor business and trade/exchange. World/global over, most industries have also awakened to the implications of environmentalism. This largely is a result of increased public awareness. The melting of the icebergs, changing temperatures in summer and winter and other such natural changes have made consumers aware of the changes happening in their environment and the reasons for the same.

CHAPTER-18 - STORE DESIGN, LAYOUT AND VISUAL MERCHANDISING

SUMMARY

LO1 Design is fast becoming a differentiating factor in retail. The store design and layout tell a customer what the store is all about. It is a very strong tool in the hands of the retailer for communicating and creating the image of the store in the mind of the customers. It is the creation of this image that is the starting point of all marketing efforts.

LO 2 The principles of store design, include totality, which means that the entre store has to be conceived as one unit which draws upon the retailer's very reason for existence store has to come across as one entity. The second principle is of Focus, where in while aspiring to create beautiful places for the consumer to shop in the retailer should not forget that the primary focus within the store has to be the product or the merchandise. The third principle is of Ease of Shopping which entails that the store has to be easy for the customer to navigate, easy to access and most importantly simple to understand. The last principle is of Change and Flexibility which have to be considered from the point of the ever-changing consumer needs and store design has to be adaptable to that change.

L0 3 The exterior look of the store and the store interiors both play an important role, the exterior look of the store draws a customer to the store-it is the first impression that a customer has of the store. It is a function of the location of the store site, which is a combination of various factors like the site itself, facilities like parking and the ease of access. The architecture of the building is a combination of the frontage and exterior of the building, the display space and the health and safety provisions provided. Health and safety standards may not really because of concern for Indian retailers, however, they are an important factor internationally.

LO 4 Store interiors is a function of the fixtures, flooring, ceiling, lighting and signages used within the store to create the look. Integral to the interior look of the store is the layout of the store. A layout is like a plan for the store. It is meant to aid movement and flow of customers, so that they move through the entire store. Store layouts may be classified as grid, racetrack or freeform.

An important element of a store layout is space planning. Space planning helps a retailer determine the amount of space available for selling and for storage. It is not only an element of retail design but is also an element of merchandise management/ category management. Since category /merchandise managers are responsible for the overall profitability of the merchandise, it is linked to the retail space allocated for the merchandise within the store.

LO 5,6 Visual merchandising is the orderly, systematic, logical and intelligent way of displaying merchandise in the retail store. To produce good visual merchandising, it is vital to understand the product and the customer. Colours and textures, props and fixture, store windows, the instore lighting and mannequins are the key tools use in merchandising.

Review questions

1. What is a 'store design? What is its significance in modern retail?
Ans- Design is fast becoming a differentiating factor in retail. The store design and layout tells a customer what the store is all about. It is a very strong tool in the hands of the retailer for communicating and creating the image of the store in the mind of the customers. It is the creation of this image that is the starting point of all marketing efforts.

2. What are the principles of store design?
Ans- The principles of store design, include totality, which means that the entre store has to be conceived as one unit which draws upon the retailer's very reason for existence store has to come across as one entity. The second principle is of Focus, where in while aspiring to create beautiful places for the consumer to shop in the retailer should not forget that the primary focus within the store has to be the product

or the merchandise. The third principle is of Ease of Shopping which entails that the store has to be easy for the customer to navigate, easy to access and most importantly simple to understand. The last principle is of Change and Flexibility which have to be considered from the point of the ever-changing consumer needs and store design has to be adaptable to that change.

3. What are the elements of store design?

Ans- The exterior look of the store and the store interiors both play an important role, the exterior look of the store draws a customer to the store-it is the first impression that a customer has of the store. It is a function of the location of the store site, which is a combination of various factors like the site itself, facilities like parking and the ease of access. The architecture of the building is a combination of the frontage and exterior of the building, the display space and the health and safety provisions provided. Health and safety standards may not really because of concern for Indian retailers, however, they are an important factor internationally.

4. Discuss the role of atmospherics in store design.

Ans- Atmospherics are the controllable characteristics of retail space which entice customers to enter the store, shop, and point of purchase. Many retail giants will use elements of atmospherics to help identify their retail brand and set it apart from competitors.

5. Discuss the layout that would be suitable for a supermarket and a department store.

Ans- An important element of a store layout is space planning. Space planning helps a retailer determine the amount of space available for selling and for storage. It is not only an element of retail design but is also an element of merchandise management/ category management. Since category /merchandise managers are responsible for the overall profitability of the merchandise, it is linked to the retail space allocated for the merchandise within the store.

6. Explain the following terms:
(a) Visual merchandising
(b) Planograms
(c) Circulation Plan
(d) Graphics and signages

Answers
(a) Visual merchandising
Visual merchandising is the orderly, systematic, logical and intelligent way of displaying merchandise in the retail store. To produce good visual merchandising, it is vital to understand the product and the customer. Colours and textures, props and fixture, store windows, the instore lighting and mannequins are the key tools use in merchandising.

(b) Planograms
A planogram is a visual merchandising tool. Planograms are detailed drawings of your store layout with special attention on product placement. Merriam-Webster defines it as such: "a schematic drawing or plan for displaying merchandise in a store so as to maximize sales."

(c) Circulation Plan
Circulation plans are used by i.e. by city planners and other officials (such as county planning officials). to manage and monitor traffic and pedestrian patterns in such a way that they might discover how to make future improvements to the system

(d) Graphics and signages
Retail Store Signage Design refers to any kind of visual store graphics that you have that displays information to your customers about your business and your products

CHAPTER-19 - MANAGING RETAIL INFRASTRUCTURE

SUMMARY

LO I The growth of malls in India can be attributed to the growth in organized retail in the country/nation. The urban mall has a local counterpart in the hats and melas which have existed and will continue to exist in various parts of the country/nation. A growing economy along with a fast pace of urbanization, favorable demographics have helped the growth of the Indian retail market.

LO 2 The key element to be considered while developing a mall is to consider for whom the mall is being developed, i.e. who is the target audience. This element of analysis would have to be considered with the location of the mall itself. The accessibility of the site for shoppers also needs to be studied and the amenities that will be provided in terms of parking have to be taken into account, An understanding of the catchment area enables the management to understand and estimate the possible footfalls and possible spending pattern in the mail, estimating the possible footfalls and spend. The development of a mall also requires substantial financial investments on the part of the developer.

LO 3,4 A key aspect of the success of the mall is the tenant mix, which typically comprises of the anchor tenant/s and the other tenants. The anchor tenant/s is typically the main reason for the customers to be drawn to the mall. Retail mall developers may need to evaluate the attractiveness of certain markets in India, and accordingly adapt their strategies to the same. The tenant and the facilities mix in a mall may also be evaluated as one evaluates a product portfolio.

The development of shopping centers has to synchronies with retail development in the country/nation. In India, while the retail sector may have crossed the initial phase and moved into the second phase of development, mall development has moved faster. For a country/nation as diverse as India, one needs to consider various options for catering to a wide section of the audience.

KEY TERMS

1. Retail development
2. Accessibility
3. Shopping mall
4. Economic development
5. Mall management
6. Financial viability
7. Catchment area
8. Tenant mix

Review questions

1. Can a break-even analysis be done for a mall, and what are the factors that would go into analyzing the mall economics in a major metro in India and in tier II and tier III cities?

Ans- The growth of malls in India can be attributed to the growth in organized retail in the country/nation. The urban mall has a local counterpart in the haats and melas which have existed and will continue to exist in various parts of the country/nation. A growing economy along with a fast pace of urbanization, favorable demographics have helped the growth of the Indian retail market.

The development of shopping centers has to synchronies with retail development in the country/nation. In India, while the retail sector may have crossed the initial phase and moved into the second phase of development, mall development has moved faster. For a country/nation as diverse as India, one needs to consider various options for catering to a wide section of the audience.

2. What can be termed as 'critical success factors' for a mall in India?

Ans- Location The location of the mall is of foremost importance as it is directly related to the catchment of the mall. Catchment refers to the type of customers and their purchasing power. Therefore, better location implies better catchment. Catchment further helps in filtering the brands that would perform in that location. Overall, identifying the right location with respect to the target audience and their spending habits are the precursors to the success of the mall.

Innovative Design
India has surpassed the nascent stage of retailing. Now, the customers not only look for quality brands and adequate facilities and services under one roof but also wish to experience state-of-the-art design and architecture. Therefore, a mall should be architecturally uniform, well-designed and developed for commercial use, and well-integrated with different types and sizes of stores to tailor the needs of the given catchment area.

Strong Catchment
Catchment analysis is utmost essential in the success of a retail hub. It not only helps in identifying the potential customer base in any geographical area but also aids in deciding an ideal location. However, catchment analysis for a mall is subject to various geo-demographic factors such as occupation, native language, the educational standard which aids in understanding customer preferences, buying potential, purchase intentions and the likelihood of buying the group of products. On the whole, catchment study provides an idea about the number of customers anticipated to visit the store and the product that would witness demand.

Appropriate Tenant Mix
An appropriate tenant mix and the location of the mall play a crucial role in determining the success of the mall. Therefore, which brands to rope in requires adequate research of market trends and catchment's behavior. By definition, tenant mix is the combination of heterogeneous and homogeneous retail agglomerations that embolden better relationship between customers and retail activities.

Parking
Shopping centers' earn their significant share of turnover from parking. Thus, the size of their parking area has a direct bearing on the store-types and sales. A shopping centre should provide sufficient parking space to lure customers. Lack of parking on holidays or weekends, particularly for car owners may turn off customers and drive them to competitors. Besides comfort, ample parking space ensures and reduces traffic improving the overall brand image of the mall. Conclusively, the right strategy and adequate market research are essential for the success of a mall in India.

With huge diversity, the above factors should be thoroughly evaluated to ensure higher Return on Investment.

3. What are the future challenges that would be faced by mall developers?
Ans- Growing e-commerce

The average share of e-commerce in Europe has been growing year-after-year reaching its current high at 9%. There are no signs of this development turning or even slowing down. Not at all. The UK has the highest share of e-commerce. In 2016 e-commerce made out 15.2% of all retail turnover in the UK. It is estimated that the number has increased to 17.8% in 2017. This means that UK consumers are spending an estimated €76 billion online in 2017. This is turnover that goes straight to the retailers with an online presence, whether or not they have brick-and-mortar stores in shopping malls.

Lack of customer insights

Online retailers have the advantage of a range of unique customer insights. They know who their customers are down to each individual. They know what attracts different customer segments, how often they visit and what they buy. The comprehensive opportunities to gain customer insights enable the online retailers to communicate in a personal and relevant way with each individual customer, thereby increasing the impact and returns of their marketing budgets. Compared to online retailers, shopping malls typically have very limited customer insights. They typically work with revenue numbers in totals or on a categorical level combined with visit counting hardware measuring the number of visitors but gather very little information about characteristics of the different visitors. Revenue and visitor counts are important indicators of how well the malls are performing, but it can be hard to convert the indicators to insights about how to improve their communication with their different customers, which is extremely important to make sure customers keeps coming back in the future to shop in their local shopping mall.

Marketing channels are losing impact

A lack of customer insight limits the opportunities to be sufficiently relevant in the communication with customers. This is an important explanation of why traditional marketing channels are losing impact. Shopping malls, who have not yet managed to adjust their marketing mix to allow for the use of data driven marketing channels, are now at risk of facing a decrease in visitor count and revenue. A study made for a Scandinavian shopping mall with 110 stores measuring the impact of a traditional printed magazine shows that the mall pays more than €66 per customer influenced by the magazine to visit the mall with an intention of buying. With an average basket size of €37 per customer in the mall, the business case is far from satisfying.

4. What are the long-term benefits of creating and positioning a mall as a brand? How can this be achieved?

Ans- Shopping malls contribute to business more significantly than traditional markets, which are viewed as a simple convergence of supply and demand. Shopping malls attract buyers and sellers, and attract customers, providing enough time to make choices as well as a recreational means of shopping. However, competition between malls, congestion of markets and traditional shopping centers has led mall developers and management to consider alternative methods to build excitement in customers. This study examines the impact of growing congestion of shopping malls in urban areas on shopping convenience and shopping behavior. Based on the survey of urban shoppers, the study analyses the cognitive attributes of the shoppers towards attractiveness of shopping malls and intensity of shopping. The results of the study reveal that the ambience of shopping malls, assortment of stores, sales promotions and comparative economic gains in the malls attract higher customer traffic to the malls.

CHAPTER-20 - SUPPLY CHAIN MANAGEMENT

SUMMARY

LO 1,2 A supply chain is a network of facilities and distribution options that performs the functions of procurement of materials, transformation of these materials into intermediate and finished products, and the distribution of these products to the customers. The challenge of managing a continuous supply of goods from all these different entities is the challenge of managing the supply chain.

LO 3 The concept of supply chain management first emerged in the United States of America, through the efforts of the apparel industry/sector. Its application and benefits-initiated grocery retailers to adapt to the concept of Efficient Consumer Response.

LO 4,5 The retailer needs to evolve the supply chain at the strategic level, the structural level and at a functional level. This includes developing policies and procedures around the facilities and equipment to be deployed, implementing information systems to support the operations and ensuring that the right organization/companyal and training inputs are provided. The concept of an agile supply chain is fast emerging and requires a great deal of integration between all the elements of the supply chain. The complexity within the supply chain varies from industry/sector to industry/sector. The nature of the industry/sector that the retail organization/company operates in also influences supply chain and logistics decisions.

LO 6 An integral part of Supply Chain Management is Logistics Management. The main objective of logistics management is to reduce inventory-holding costs and improve profits. Logistics is derived from the French word 'loger', which means to quarter and supply troops. A logistics system has to be built to suit the needs to the organization/company keeping in mind the kind of products that company retails and the competition prevailing.

KEY TERMS

1. Supply chain management
2. Quick response
3. Time-to-market
4. Time-to-serve
5. Supply chain integration
6. Collaborative planning
7. Forecasting and replenishment
8. Third party logistics provider
9. Reverse logistics
10. Time-to-react
11. Vendor managed inventory
12. Retail logistics
13. Fourth party logistics

Review questions

1. What is 'supply chain management? What are the reasons for the emergence of supply chain management?

Ans- A supply chain is a network of facilities and distribution options that performs the functions of procurement of materials, transformation of these materials into intermediate and finished products, and the distribution of these products to the customers. The challenge of managing a continuous supply of goods from all these different entities is the challenge of managing the supply chain.

The concept of supply chain management first emerged in the United States of America, through the efforts of the apparel industry/sector. Its application and benefits initiated grocery retailers to adapt to the concept of Efficient Consumer Response.

2. What is supply chain integration, and why is it relevant to retail organization/companys?

Ans- An integral part of Supply Chain Management is Logistics Management. The main objective of logistics management is to reduce inventory-holding costs and improve profits. Logistics is derived from the French word 'loger', which means to quarter and supply troops.

3. What is retail logistics?
Ans-. A logistics system has to be built to suit the needs to the organization/company keeping in mind the kind of products that company retails and the competition prevailing.

4. Why is the concept of reverse logistics gaining importance?
Ans- Reverse logistics are the means to having an efficient supply chain and, therefore, efficient asset recovery. Here are a few reasons why reverse logistics are so crucial to business: Reverse logistics provide a way to extract the maximum value from products at the end of their life cycle.

5. Explain the terms:
(a) Time to market
(b) Lead time gap
(c) Collaborative Planning Forecasting and Replenishment
(d) Cross Docking

Answers
(a)Time to market
In commerce, time to market (TTM) is the length of time it takes from a product being conceived until its being available for sale. The reason that time to market is so important is because being late erodes the addressable market that you have to sell your product into. A common assumption is that TTM matters most for first-of-a-kind products, but actually a late product launch in any industry/sector can negatively impact revenues—from reducing the window of opportunity to generate revenues to causing the product to become obsolete faster.

(b) Lead time gap
Lead time gap the difference between logistics **lead time** and the customer's order **cycle time** is called **lead time gap**. **lead time gap** = logistics **lead time** - customers order **cycle** time where, logistics **lead** time = total **time** to complete the manufacturing and product.

(c) Collaborative Planning Forecasting and Replenishment

Collaborative Planning, Forecasting and Replenishment (CPFR) is an approach which aims to enhance supply chain integration by supporting and assisting joint practices. CPFR seeks cooperative management of inventory through joint visibility and replenishment of products throughout the supply chain. Information shared between suppliers and retailers aids in planning and satisfying customer demands through a supportive system of shared information. This allows for continuous updating of inventory and upcoming requirements, making the end-to-end supply chain process more efficient. Efficiency is created through the decrease expenditures for merchandising, inventory, logistics, and transportation across all trading partners.

(d) Cross Docking

Cross docking is a logistics procedure where products from a supplier or manufacturing plant are distributed directly to a customer or retail chain with marginal to no handling or storage time.

CHAPTER-21 - UNDERSTANDING RETAIL VIABILITY

SUMMARY

LO 1 The success of retail depends on two key issues: the ability to manage costs and the ability to manage assets. There are three main costs involved in the retail business. The first is the cost of procuring merchandise, the second is the cost of sales and the third is the investment in the land or the lease for the store.

The concept of retail economics covers the planning for new ventures. New ventures may be the completely new ventures that the retailer is entering into like new business areas or new geographical markets. Financial planning may also be needed for acquiring an existing business, for expansion. The primary tool used for assessing whether a retailer should venture into new markets or business areas is a Feasibility Report.

LO2 The income statement is a record of the revenues earned by an organization/company and the expenses incurred. Income statement is the snapshot of a company's operational performance for a particular period of time. It takes the company's revenues and expenses arid gives profits as output.

LO3 Ratio analysis is the most commonly used analysis to judge the financial strength of a company. Ratio analysis is not just comparing different numbers from the balance sheet, income statement, and cash flow statement. It is comparing the number against previous years, other companies, the industry/sector, or even the economy in general. Ratios look at the relationships between individual values and relate them to how a company has performed in the past, and might perform in the future.

LO 4 The balance sheet and the income statement are corporate measures of financial performance. The Strategic Profit Model is a combination of both the measures. It combines the information provided by the balance sheet and the income statement into one comprehensive model and is based on three Important financial ratios of the Net Profit Margin, the Asset Turnover Ratio and the Return on Assets.

KEY TERMS

1. Retail economics
2. Feasibility report
3. Measures of performance
4. Income statement
5. Cost of goods sold
6. Gross margin
7. Balance sheet
8. Gross profit margin
9. Operating expenses
10. Net profit margin
11. Current ratio
12. Return on capital employed
13. GMROI
14. GMROF

Review questions

1. What are the drivers of cost in the retail industry/sector?

Ans- The success of retail depends on two key issues: the ability to manage costs and the ability to manage assets. There are three main costs involved in the retail business. The first is the cost of procuring merchandise, the second is the cost of sales and the third is the investment in the land or the lease for the store.

The concept of retail economics covers the planning for new ventures. New ventures may be the completely new ventures that the retailer is entering into like new business areas or new geographical markets. Financial planning may also be needed for acquiring an existing business, for expansion. The primary tool used for assessing whether a retailer should venture into new markets or business areas is a Feasibility Report.

2. What aspects of performance does the typical retailer measure?
Ans The income statement is a record of the revenues earned by an organization/company and the expenses incurred. Income statement is the snapshot of a company's operational performance for a particular period of time. It takes the company's revenues and expenses arid gives profits as output.

3. What are some of the measures and metrics that are commonly used by the retailer to monitor performance?

Ans- Foot Traffic

Diving deeper into foot traffic is beneficial, as this important KPI sets the stage for numerous sales-related metrics inside the store. Maintaining an ongoing tally of foot traffic, or customers who actually walk through your door, helps you to gauge your marketing and advertising campaigns' effectiveness. Door traffic can also provide clues on your window displays' appeal.

• **How to measure your foot traffic**

The most effective way to measure foot traffic is to use people counters such as thermal sensors, video cameras, break beams, Wi-Fi, or Bluetooth Beacons.
The right foot traffic solution depends on your needs, and you should consider factors such as the cost of the solution, the implementation process, and the types of data that you can extract. The best people counting solutions are the ones that deliver tremendous insights while still remaining cost-effective.

• **How to improve your foot traffic**

Next, build relationships with your customers (and prospects) through e-Newsletters, social media campaigns, and other online venues. Through these ongoing contacts, shoppers will be encouraged to keep your store "top of mind" when searching for products they want.

Units per Transaction

Your store's Units per Transaction (also known as Average Items per Transaction) is one of retail's most important key metrics. It shows **the average number of items customers buy in a specific transaction**. A higher Units per Transaction (UPT) means customers are piling more items in their carts during each visit. This desirable outcome means customers are enjoying their shopping experience, and are staying long enough to buy more items than they initially intended. It's also an indicator that your store understands its customer base, and offers products that shopper's value. In some cases, your UPT could shed light on how effective your sales techniques are. When people are buying more items per visit, it could indicate that your associates are doing a great job at cross-selling and product recommendations.

- **How to measure units per transaction**

Finding the Units per Transaction requires a simple calculation:
Units per Transaction = Total Number of Items Bought / Number of Transactions
Example: If a retail store sold a total of 342 items and processed 119 transactions in a given month, then the business would calculate its UPT of the month as follows:
342 / 119 = 2.87 units per transaction

- **How to improve units per transaction**

To raise this KPI, set the stage for customers to purchase additional items during a single shopping trip. Place add-on products near items that customers are likely to purchase. If it's economically feasible, add more color and/or style choices to a popular clothing line. Consider incentive pricing that may spur customers to buy multiples of a specific product.

Sales per Employee

Tracking your retail store's Sales per Employee gives you a running snapshot of your sales associates' performance. **This data can help you in planning work schedules and sales incentives.** Over time, you'll notice opportunities for training and individual recognition.

- **How to measure sales per employee**

Track your sales per employee with this simple formula:
Sales per Employee = Net Sales / Number of Employees
Example: If a retailer has 4 employees and a net sale of $11,500 then its sales per employee would be:
$11,500 / 4 = $2,875 per employee
If you have a POS system that gives each employee a sign-in code, you can easily track that associate's daily, weekly, and monthly sales. By gathering that data, you'll gain clues to your employees' overall performance.

- **How to improve sales per employee**

Although there's no universal solution to getting your employees to sell more products, **setting individual goals for each associate is a good start.**
Create an incentive system that will motivate employees to up their games. Providing relevant sales training through videos and role-playing may also be helpful.

Sales per Square Foot
Sales per square foot is exactly what it sounds like: it's a measure of the revenue generated per square foot of sales space in your store.
To grasp this KPI's full impact, think of your store's sales floor as a powerful engine that drives the business' success. For the engine to run at maximum efficiency, **every square foot of sales space must pull its weight,** or generate enough revenue to enable you to meet preset operational goals.

- **How to measure sales per square foot**

Maximizing your Sales per Square Foot means earning the highest possible revenue from each square foot of sales space. Here's the simple formula:
Sales per Square Foot = Net Sales / Total Sales Floor Space
Example: A store with 2,100 square feet of selling space and net sales of $155,000 would have the following calculation:
$155,000 / 2,100 = $73.80 per square foot

- **How to improve sales per square foot**

To beef up your numbers, examine the weekly, monthly, quarterly, and yearly trends for each product or sales floor segment. When you find underperforming products or product classes, revamp your displays and retool your marketing and advertising programs.

Consider moving those lagging products to another part of the sales floor, as customers could be ignoring them in their current location. If you've made all those moves and your efforts haven't paid off, hold a blowout sale to help cut your losses.

During your next store redesign, introduce products that may better resonate with your customers.

4. Discuss the importance and feasibility of aligning performance of the individual employee to that of the store/organization/company.

Ans- Grow your company from within.

- When searching for ways to improve your organization/company, in many situations, the best place to start is from within.
- When executed properly, improvements within your company can be beneficial for driving performance and encouraging employee progress.
- Be engaging, learn the metrics, utilize training methods and place a focus on the business; all of these are simple ways to improve your organization/company.

Organization/companyal improvements are an ongoing process, and each organization/company has its own specific needs; however, there are common improvements that are necessary for many organization/companys on an ongoing basis, including:

- **Strategy and mission:** Changes in strategy and mission are often difficult to map out, but, as a business owner, you need to continually monitor how well – or if – your organization/company is meeting your mission, and you need to be prepared to change strategies if needed.

- **Organization/companyal structure:** This concerns the roles, objectives, and responsibilities of individuals, departments, and teams. Structures change, some are relatively minor, while some such as mergers are considered extreme and intense.

- **People:** Organization/companyal improvements in regards to personnel consist of turnover, hiring, training and other changes that will be beneficial for the organization/company.

- **Knowledge:** Changes/improvements to the knowledge of an organization/company is critical for process, progress and initiative.

It's a fact that the pace of change is so fast that mergers and acquisitions are on the rise as one of the best ways of achieving strategic growth. What if you're not ready or willing to merge or be acquired by another business? Check out the six steps to grow your business from within.

In our sluggish economy, a multitude of mergers and acquisitions notwithstanding, the capacity for a business to grow rests in the hands of its people.

CEOs throughout the world/global are driving to improving organization/companyal performance regardless of size or industry/sector. Much has been written and studied on this subject, and we find in myriad of surveys and books that there are six steps that, executed effectively, drive performance improvement and growth capacity.

Engage your people.

Employee engagement is one of the most written and talked about issues today in business. Below are key actions you, as a business owner, can take to enable your people to engage: to feel passionate about the work they do, deliver their best performance and to strengthen their commitment:

- Build a strong understanding of your business strategy throughout your workforce. Ensure everyone can answer the following questions: Why do customers buy from us? Who are our key competitors, and why do their customers buy from them? How do I contribute to our unique differentiation?

- Build trust. Employees need to know that their managers and executives care about them as people as well as being committed to their success.

- Make sure every employee is using his or her preferred skills and has an effective degree of autonomy.

- Focus each department on improving its procedures and targeting its activities on better achieving the company's competitive differentiation through what people do and how they do it.

Leverage high-impact leadership practices.

Communication is king in today's organization/companys. It's one of the biggest challenges' leaders have and is probably a weakness for many companies. Communicate clearly in simple language, creatively, interactively, daily about core business subjects, such as:

- Departmental and organization/company performance targets, progress, obstacles and solutions

- Stories about competitors and customer successes, i.e., from sales and customer service

- Current organization/companyal initiatives

Identify and remove internal roadblocks.

How well aligned with your competitive differentiation strategy are your company's policies, procedures and structure? Look for indicators of misalignment such as:

- Do people need to work around policies and work procedures to get things done?

- Do your policies and work procedures enable people to get the right things done quickly?

- How are relationships between functions, i.e., manufacturing and sales? Are conflicts and frustrations routine?

Align your metrics.

To have meaning, the metrics people focus on need to be understood by them to be within their influence. Here's how metrics can help each department help your company meet is goals:

- Your metrics can provide great value when they serve as a guide to decision-making and prioritizing work.
- Nonfinancial metrics that relate directly to your competitive differentiation can help keep everyone aligned in a similar strategic direction.
- Explaining how metrics are chosen and measured and tailoring metrics to each department can enable people to understand how they each make a difference in the company's performance.

CHAPTER-22 – RETAIL MARKETING AND BRANDING

SUMMARY

LO 1 Retail marketing focuses on the segmentation, targeting, positioning and branding of a retail store and the methods of communicating this to the consumer. The marketing tools that a retail organization uses to pursue its marketing objectives are termed as the retail marketing mix.

LO 2 The components of the retail marketing mix are Product, Price, Place, Promotion, Presentation, People and Customer Service. The retail marketing mix is used to develop an appropriate marketing strategy for the store depending on the target market to be serviced. Markets are large and varied and so are the needs of the customers. The marketing strategy evolved as a result of segmentation, targeting and positioning commonly known as STP marketing. The segment, target market and the positioning strategy adopted by the retailer dictates the image to be created for a retail store. This, in turn, decides the communication mix that the retailer chooses to communicate with the consumers.

Communication is an integral part of the retailer's marketing strategy. Primarily communication is used to inform the customers about the retailer, the merchandise and the services. It also serves as a tool for building the store image. The retailer can use various platforms/channels for communication. The most common tools are Advertising, Sales Promotion, Public Relations, Publicity and Personal Selling.

LO 3 Communication is an integral part of the retailer's marketing strategy. Primarily communication is used to inform the customers about the retailer, the merchandise and the services. It also serves as a tool for building the store image. Retail communication has moved on from the time when the retailer alone communicated with the consumers. Today consumers can communicate or reach the organization/companys. The main media used for advertising are press, television, radio, cinema, posters, hoardings, and direct mail. Advertising may also be done on bus shelters, buses, road dividers, kiosks, balloons, etc. The kind of media vehicle chosen by the retailer largely depends on the reach of that particular medium to the target audience.

LO 4 The need for a synergy between the messages being sent out to the target audience, gave rise to the concept of Integrated Marketing Communications (IMC). IMC is a concept that is designed to make all aspects of marketing communication such as advertising, sales promotion, public relations, and direct marketing work together as a unified force, rather than permitting each to work in isolation.

LO 5 As markets evolve and become more competitive it will become more important for retailers to focus on branding. Retail branding does not necessarily focus only on the creation of a private label alone. In case of multi brand retailers the task becomes more difficult as the retailer needs to create a store identity, which is different from that of the brands that he sells within the store, but at the same time there has to be a level of consistency among the products available.

Brands, which fail to deliver, might not see the light of another day. The key to success is building experiences, which retain the customers and make them talk about it. Successful branding would be about delivering, products and experiences to the customer and making him talk about it. The concept of 360-degree branding is about influencing "everything a consumer experience".

KEY TERMS

1. Consumerism
2. Retail
3. Marketing
4. Breadth
5. Depth
6. Retail positioning
7. Marketing mix
8. Target market
9. Advertising
10. Segmentation
11. Retail image
12. Direct marketing
13. Sales promotion
14. Public relations
15. Personal selling
16. Point of purchase
17. Integrated marketing
18. Communication

Review Questions

1. Explain the components of the "Retail Marketing Mix."

Ans- Retail marketing focuses on the segmentation, targeting, positioning and branding of a retail store and the methods of communicating this to the consumer. The marketing tools that a retail organization/company uses to pursue its marketing objectives are termed as the retail marketing mix.

2. How would the communication mix vary for a supermarket and for a department store?

Ans- Communication is an integral part of the retailer's marketing strategy. Primarily communication is used to inform the customers about the retailer, the merchandise and the services. It also serves as a tool for building the store image. Retail communication has moved on from the time when the retailer alone communicated with the consumers. Today consumers can communicate or reach the organization/companys. The main media used for advertising are press, television, radio, cinema, posters, hoardings, and direct mail. Advertising may also be done on bus shelters, buses, road dividers, kiosks, balloons, etc. The kind of media vehicle chosen by the retailer largely depends on the reach of that particular medium to the target audience.

3. What do you understand by the term 'retail image? Does a good retail image necessarily mean a strong brand value?

Ans The components of the retail marketing mix are Product, Price, Place, Promotion, Presentation, People and Customer Service. The retail marketing mix is used to develop an appropriate marketing strategy for the store depending on the target market to be serviced. Markets are large and varied and so are the needs of the customers. The marketing strategy evolved as a result of segmentation, targeting and positioning commonly known as STP marketing. The segment, target market and the positioning strategy adopted by the retailer dictates the image to be created for a retail store. This, in turn, decides the communication mix that the retailer chooses to communicate with the consumers.

Communication is an integral part of the retailer's marketing strategy. Primarily communication is used to inform the customers about the retailer, the merchandise and the services. It also serves as a tool for building the store image. The retailer can use various platforms/channels for communication. The most common tools are Advertising, Sales Promotion, Public Relations, Publicity and Personal Selling.

4. What is the role of POP in retail?

Ans- A point of purchase (**POP**) is a term used by marketers and **retailers** when planning the placement of consumer products, such as product displays strategically placed in a grocery **store** aisle or advertised in a weekly flyer.

5. What is the significance of branding in retail?

Ans- As markets evolve and become more competitive it will become more important for retailers to focus on branding. Retail branding does not necessarily focus only on the creation of a private label alone. In case of multi brand retailers the task becomes more difficult as the retailer needs to create a store identity, which is different from that of the brands that he sells within the store, but at the same time there has to be a level of consistency among the products available.

Brands, which fail to deliver, might not see the light of another day. The key to success is building experiences, which retain the customers and make them talk about it. Successful branding would be about delivering, products and experiences to the customer and making him talk about it. The concept of 360-degree branding is about influencing "everything a consumer experience".

CHAPTER-23 - SERVICING THE RETAIL CUSTOMER

SUMMARY

LO 1 Retail is a part of the service sector. The world/global has moved on from the age of customer satisfaction to the age of customer delight and organization/company are remodeling their strategies around the customer and his needs with the aim of bringing him back and keeping him for life.

LO 2, LO3 The concepts of customer service and customer satisfaction need to be understood. Very often the terms customer service and customer satisfaction are used interchangeably, however the basic difference between them needs to be understood. "Customer service" focuses on measurement of how well a firm meets the performance standards that are viewed as important to meeting customers' needs. "Customer satisfaction" on the other hand, is how the customers measure the service performance of a firm.

Customer service has today become an integral part of the retail industry/sector. Creating a superior service level requires that the organization/company:

1. Identify the key customers and listen and respond to them.

2. Define superior service and establish a service strategy.

3. Set Standards and Measure Performance.

4. Select, train and empower employees to work for the customer.

5, Recognize and reward accomplishment.

While customer service has become an imminently necessary part of the retail trade/exchange, it is equally necessary to evaluate the service quality provided. Customer service is largely a function of perception, customer expectations and the service actually provided. Dissatisfaction with services provided largely stems from a difference between expectations and what is actually provided. This is the basic premise for understanding the gaps that may arise in customer service.

LO 4, LO 5 Retailers use various methods and programmes for obtaining information on customers and their level of satisfaction. Retailers also use various tools to encourage loyalty. One such tool is the customer loyalty card devised by retailers. Customer Relationship Management (CRM) is a tool for servicing the consumer. CRM aims at creating customers for life and tries to secure a share of the mind thereby, creating market share and a share of the wallet for the organization/company. The concept of CRM has special relevance in retail, if used effectively; it can add value to the offering made by the retailer.

LO 6 The retail salesperson plays a key role in the service provided by the retail firm. He represents the store to the consumers and communicates customer feedback to the management. The retailing process requires researching customer preferences, developing value propositions, establishing retail networks and supply chains, setting up stores, filling it up with merchandise and getting the customers in to buy the merchandise.

KEY TERMS
1. Customer service
2. Customer satisfaction
3. Moments of truth
4. The standards gap
5. Gaps in service
6. The delivery gap
7. Customer Relationship management
8. Personal selling
9. The knowledge gap
10. The communications gap
11. Loyalty cards
12. Retail selling process

Review Questions

1. What is the significance of service to a retailer?

Ans- Retail is a part of the service sector. The world/global has moved on from the age of customer satisfaction to the age of customer delight and organization/company are remodeling their strategies around the customer and his needs with the aim of bringing him back and keeping him for life.

2. How can gaps in service be identified? Specify giving examples.

Ans- The customer service has become an imminently necessary part of the retail trade/exchange; it is equally necessary to evaluate the service quality provided. Customer service is largely a function of perception, customer expectations and the service actually provided. Dissatisfaction with services provided largely stems from a difference between expectations and what is actually provided. This is the basic premise for understanding the gaps that may arise in customer service.

3. How do large national retailers target improvement in customer service using loyal programmes?

Ans- The concepts of customer service and customer satisfaction need to be understood. Very often the terms customer service and customer satisfaction are used interchangeably, however the basic difference between them needs to be understood. "Customer service" focuses on measurement of how well a firm meets the performance standards that are viewed as important to meeting customers' needs. "Customer satisfaction" on the other hand, is how the customers measure the service performance of a firm.

Customer service has today become an integral part of the retail industry/sector. Creating a superior service level requires that the organization/company:

1. Identify the key customers and listen and respond to them.

2. Define superior service and establish a service strategy.

3. Set Standards and Measure Performance.

4. Select, train and empower employees to work for the customer.

5, Recognize and reward accomplishment.

4. What is 'service blueprinting'? Why it is critical in retail

Ans- The **service blueprint** is a diagram/ map that visualizes a service offering accurately. It provides a clear picture of the service process to those who are involved in service production as well as service consumption.

CHAPTER-24 - ROLE OF TECHNOLOGY IN RETAIL

SUMMARY

LO 1 The retail business is an early adapter of Information Technology (IT). The importance of information technology in retail stems from the importance of data. Data is nothing but information, which aids decision-making. The right data, in the right form to the right set of people at the right time, is one of the greatest tools in the hands of the retailer. Information is always with reference to a particular time-frame. The use of information technology in retail includes software, hardware and wire line and wireless communication. Typically, a mature user of IT in retail uses a number of technologies such as: POS terminals, software for managing inventory and for interaction at various levels, The industry/sector uses technology applications like EDI, data warehousing / mining for trend analysis and customer management and highly specialized solutions for Supply Chain Management

LO 2 The Universal Product Code or the bar code is basically a product identifier, made up of a series of bars and spaces, which represent alphanumeric information. In 1972, manufacturers and distributors of 12 European countries formed a council to explore the development of a standard numbering system for Europe, similar to and compatible with the UPC. The European Article Numbering (EAN) was born as a result. It is a superset of the UPC and is followed in India.

LO 3 While every retailer may want to harness the power of technology and use it to its optimum advantage, many factors affect its use. The chief among them are, the scale and scope of operations, the financial resources available to the organization/company, the nature of the business and the human resources available

LO 4 Technology enables efficient stocking of merchandise, collection of data on consumer preferences and purchases, and efficiency in operations. The scale at which a retailer may use technology depends on the size and scale of operations, the financial resources available, the nature of business and the human resources available to implement the technology solutions.

KEY TERMS

1. Universal product code
2. Bar code and European article numbering
3. Data mining
4. Data warehousing
5. Radio frequency
6. Electronic data interchange
7. identification
8. Database management

Review Questions

1. Identify the benefits from an integrated IT solution supporting the retail business.
Ans- The retail business is an early adapter of Information Technology (IT). The importance of information technology in retail stems from the importance of data. Data is nothing but information, which aids decision-making. The right data, in the right form to the right set of people at the right time, is one of the greatest
tools in the hands of the retailer. Information is always with reference to a particular time-frame.
The use of information technology in retail includes software, hardware and wire line and wireless communication. Typically, a mature user of IT in retail uses a number of technologies such as: POS terminals, software for managing inventory
and for interaction at various levels, The industry/sector uses technology applications like EDI, data warehousing / mining for trend analysis and customer management and highly specialized solutions for Supply Chain Management

2. Discuss the critical need for Common data and communication standards to support the retail industry/sector.
Ans- The Universal Product Code or the bar code is basically a product identifier, made up of a series of bars and spaces, which represent alphanumeric information. In 1972, manufacturers and distributors of 12 European countries formed a council to explore the development of a standard numbering system for Europe, similar to and compatible with the UPC. The European Article Numbering (EAN) was born as a result. It is a superset of the UPC and is followed in India.

3. Identify some of the innovations in the use of IT that the retail industry/sector has pioneered.

Ans- While every retailer may want to harness the power of technology and use it to its optimum advantage, many factors affect its use. The chief among them are, the scale and scope of operations, the financial resources available to the organization/company, the nature of the business and the human resources available

4. Which are the factors which have influenced the usage of technology in retail?

Ans- Factors that influenced the usage of technology

1. **Wearable Technology:** From headsets and smart watches to fitness and health devices, wearable technology is being embraced by shoppers for ease of accessing product and store information, offers, and speed of payment.

2. **New Retail Holidays:** Looking beyond the standard calendar, retailers are linking sales to special observances and creating their own shopping holidays to attract new buyers and engage with existing customers to boost loyalty and repeat spending.

3. **Voice Technology:** Up to four times faster than type-and-click, voice-enabled search signals a shift in how consumers find product and service information. At the same time, innovations in language recognition will give voice a bigger role in online commerce, retail search strategies, and shopper engagement.

4. **Virtual Reality (VR) in the Shopping Experience**: Virtual reality immerses consumers in sensory and personalized experiences, empowering them to interact with products and services. With mobile devices capable of delivering rich VR experiences, shoppers can tour a store or try on a new fashion anywhere, at any time.

5. **Video Streaming:** Growing video-on-demand traffic and the higher likelihood of shoppers to purchase a product after watching a video, provides opportunities for retailers to consider online streaming video for product demos, display or customer service.

6. **Internet/online of Things:** Point-of-sale information is no longer the main source of data for merchants, as millions of devices are being deployed and connected in the retail environment to collect and send data that provides valuable, real-time insights.

7. **Mobile and Alternative Payments:** Expected to increase three-fold this year, mobile payments are transforming commerce. As retailers transition terminals and develop ecommerce platforms to engage with shoppers and accept new payment methods, consumers are adopting mobile wallet apps, branded wallets, and smart watches and devices with payment capabilities.

8. **Social Network Buy Buttons**: Shopping and social media have been a natural fit, but are quickly becoming more commercial. Largely driven by growing mobile usage, retailers are providing shoppers with easier functionality to purchase within a social app by adding Buy buttons that allow users to shop directly on their sites.

9. **Increased Spending on Pets:** Pet expenditures continue to rise as consumer demographics and mindsets toward pets change. Recognizing pets are considered a member of the family more than ever, many retailers and veterinarians are focusing on the increasing demand for products and services that meet the needs of pet owners.

10. **Personalization:** All these trends intersect in the ability to deliver unique, personalized customer experiences. Data, tools and technology are making it possible to understand customer preferences and deliver personalized offerings, in addition to product selection and prices.

5. List out the prevailing applications of technology in retail.

Ans- Technology enables efficient stocking of merchandise, collection of data on consumer preferences and purchases, and efficiency in operations. The scale at which a retailer may use technology depends on the size and scale of operations, the financial resources available, the nature of business and the human resources available to implement the technology solutions.

CHAPTER-25 - THE CHANGING FACETS OF RETAIL

SUMMARY

LO 1 Technology be the key driver of the retail change and e-tailing is fast becoming an integral channel utilized by retailers as a way to reach consumers and Improve-or even just maintain-market share amidst increasing competition. The rise of the Internet/online has opened up a new avenue for retailers to reach out to customers and suppliers in markets where they may or may not have a physical presence thereby presenting opportunities for deepening customer relations, streamlining operations, cutting costs and discovering new sources of revenue. At a very broad level the business models that can be adopted for pursuing business through the electronic medium can be Electronic commerce that is conducted between businesses is referred to as business-to-business or B2B, business that is conducted between businesses and consumers and is referred to as business-to consumer or B2C. The C2C business model enables consumers to sell their assets on the website.

LO 2 Job search engines and matrimonial portals were among the early starters in the ecommerce segment in India. Growth was slow as e-Commerce in India was characterized by low internet/online penetration, a small online shopping user base, slow internet/online speed, low consumer acceptance of online shopping and inadequate logistics infrastructure. Travel emerged as the largest segment with people began relying on internet/online to search for travel-related information and to book tickets. The growth of online retail was partly driven by changing urban consumer lifestyle and the need for convenience of shopping at home.

LO3 In order to build a thriving e-business, it is necessary that the internet/online is seen as a strategic tool rather than a mere addition in terms of technology. Just as brick and mortar retailers have built brands over the years, e-tailers will need to build brands. Brand building on the web, will have to focus on the experience, as the experience will be the brand.

LO 4 What started as communication devices, have now evolved into devices that can serve many functions beyond voice communication such as taking photos and listening to music. Mobile phones are now equipped with cameras with the potential to turn them into portable bar code scanners. Recent M-Commerce developments in India include Vodafone teaming up with ICICI bank to launch M-pesa and Airtel tying up with HDFC Bank and Axis Bank for Airtel Money. E-commerce companies such as flipkart, jabong and yepme have launched mobile version of their websites. Banks like HDFC, ICICI and State Bank of India have introduced mobile version of their websites too.

LO 5,6 Multichannel retailing is not a new phenomenon, and a retailer can start from any one channel and move to other channels later. Multichannel retailing is the set of activities involved in selling merchandise or services to consumers through more than one channel. The Omni Channel approach on the other hand aims to let the customer experience all the channels in a consistent way and in a seamlessly integrated way. Technology has enabled many experience enhancers like augmented reality, Virtual shopping, and Mobile wallets which retailers are adopting to gain a competitive edge.

KEY TERMS
1. Online marketplace
2. Omni channel approach
3. Business to business
4. Business to customer
5. M-commerce
6. E-commerce
7. Augmented reality
8. Showrooming
9. Multichannel retailing
10. Webrooming

Review questions

1.What is 'ecommerce and what are the reasons for the emergence of the same?

Ans- At a very broad level the business models that can be adopted for pursuing business through the electronic medium can be Electronic commerce that is conducted between businesses is referred to as business-to-business or B2B, business that is conducted between businesses and consumers and is referred to as business-to consumer or B2C. The C2C business model enables consumers to sell their assets on the website.

Job search engines and matrimonial portals were among the early starters in the ecommerce segment in India. Growth was slow as e-Commerce in India was characterized by low internet/online penetration, a small online shopping user base, slow internet/online speed, low consumer acceptance of online shopping and inadequate logistics infrastructure. Travel emerged as the largest segment with people began relying on internet/online to search for travel-related information and to book tickets. The growth of online retail was partly driven by changing urban consumer lifestyle and the need for convenience of shopping at home.

2. Analyze the Strengths, Weaknesses, Opportunities and Threats for any two online retailers operating in India.

Ans-

Amazon SWOT Analysis:

Strengths:

Cost strategy of leadership

Services and products of higher quality

Purchase Strategic

Chain logistic and effective distribution

Weaknesses:

Only attention to online.

Selling with no profit.

Amazon new categories are damaging its brand

Opportunities:
System for paying online.
To release more its own products and services.
To increase the services and products
To open more international stores.
Threat:
Safety of online.
Strategic alliances.
Legislation counters tax.
Retailers with lower regional cost

eBay SWOT Analysis
Strengths:
Largest Internet/online market in the world/global.
Not a strong competition
Focusing on local markets
System of payment
Reputation of the mark.
Weaknesses:
High expenses.
No other strategy of growth.
Opportunities:
Increasing of mobile customers.
Becoming a retailer market.
services and product growing
Opening more international e-stores.
Threat:
Safety of being online.
Retailers with regional low cost.
Intensification of the competition of Amazon.
Rates of exchange.

3. Analyze the Indian ecommerce market with the help of the five forces model.

Ans The Ecommerce industry/sector has flourished at an impressive rate during the last few years. The reasons include growing economic activity around the world/global and the growth of technology. Both these factors have an important influence on the growth of the e-retail industry/sector. Particularly, it is in the US and Asia Pacific where the rate of growth is expected to remain the highest in the near future. Some of the major players in the industry/sector include Amazon, Ali-Baba, E-bay and Flipkart. Apart from it Walmart and Costco have also made their foray into e-retail. Moreover, the growing use of mobile technology has also proved favorable for the industry/sector and led to an increase in revenue and profits.

Bargaining power of suppliers:

In the Ecommerce industry/sector, the bargaining power of the suppliers is generally low to moderate. The reason is that the rules are set by the brand and the suppliers have to follow the code of conduct set by them. Most of the ecommerce brands are highly cautious regarding their supplier relationships and set a code of conduct related to quality, labor and wages as well as sustainability. Despite the number of players in the industry/sector having grown, the suppliers do not have too many options and therefore are bound by the rules that the brands have set. It is why the Ecommerce brands have the upper hand and the bargaining power of the suppliers is low. Some of the suppliers may have some bargaining power because of their size and quality.

Bargaining power of the buyers:

The bargaining power of the buyers is moderately high in the ecommerce industry/sector. It is because several small and big brands ha e cropped up and there is hardly any switching cost for the customers. Today's customer is well informed and has every piece of information available at a single click. Apart from it some of the physical retail brands have also entered the commerce market and the physical retail market itself adds to pressures. Most of the brands are trying very hard to retain every customer and for this purpose they make very large investments in technology and customer service. Due to all these factors the bargaining power of the buyers is moderately high the factors that can moderate their bargaining power include brand image, quality of products and service and prices.

Threat of substitute products:
There two main threats in terms of substitutes for the Ecommerce brands. The first are the competing e-retail businesses and the second are the physical retailers. Brands try to earn a competitive advantage through low prices, better quality of products or through a better overall customer experience. For the customers there are no switching costs and they can easily switch from one e-retailer to another or from ecommerce to physical retail.

Threat of new entrants:
The threat of new entrants is low to moderate in the ecommerce industry/sector. This is because there is a need for large investment in technology, human resources and marketing. The barriers to entry are moderately high. One can enter with enough capita. However, the difficulty is in terms of building brand image and trust with the customers. So, the overall threat from the new entrants gets moderated.

Rivalry in the industry/sector:
The level of rivalry in the industry/sector is high because of the large number of players. The number of local and global brands in the ecommerce market has grown and this has also led to higher competition. Apart from Amazon, Ebay, and Alibaba, there are several other local brands like Flipkart, Coles etc along with some of the retail brands like Walmart and Costco. So, the overall rivalry between these brands gets to be very high.

4. What is the need for understanding the e-marketing mix?
Ans- Helps understand what your product or service can offer to your customers. Help determine whether your product or service is suitable for your customers. Helps identify and understand the requirements of customers. Helps learn when and how to promote your product or service to your customers.

5. Discuss the scope of m-commerce in India and which are the sectors which you perceive will see faster adoption of the service.

Ans- What started as communication devices have now evolved into devices that can serve many functions beyond voice communication such as taking photos and listening to music. Mobile phones are now equipped with cameras with the potential to turn them into portable bar code scanners. Recent M-Commerce developments in India include Vodafone teaming up with ICICI bank to launch M-pesa and Airtel tying up with HDFC Bank and Axis Bank for Airtel Money. E-commerce companies such as flipkart, jabong and yepme have launched mobile version of their websites. Banks like HDFC, ICICI and State Bank of India have introduced mobile version of their websites too.

CONCLUSION

- This additional book under <u>MBA Basics in 24 Hours</u> helps you to get quick knowledge of Retail Marketing and Management brief definitions, questions/answers.
- Short, simple summary & keywords can be used to present the whole topic in just less than three hours.
- The ideas and definitions can be used for examinations, viva and also knowledge sharing/transfer.
- Group discussions can be arranged and the above chapters are really helpful to bring out the best member in management.
- Examination papers can be set at the required levels in simple terms.
- The given information in all the chapters can also be used in schools, colleges and any other levels.
- Other eight books under 'MBA Basics in 24 hours' are also given in the same way to help out best for students and tutors (published in Amazon).

  - Principles & Practices of Management
  - Human Resource Management
  - Financial Management
  - Marketing Management
  - Organisational Behaviour
  - Managerial Economics
  - Strategic Management
  - Management Information Systems

- Please follow the additional books as well!

For any feedback, query or suggestions please mail to astronara@gmail.com or info@zodiacservices.net. You can also contact via www.zodiacservices.org/contact.

THANK YOU!

www.ingramcontent.com/pod-product-compliance
Lightning Source LLC
Chambersburg PA
CBHW060855220526
45466CB00003B/1384